Vol.16
Gresley V1/
V3 &
Thompson L1
classes

Vol.21
Class A5 to
A8, H1, H2,
L1(L3), L2,
M1 & M2
Tank Engines

The Gresley
N1 & N2 Tank
Engines

Vol.17
Class B13,
B14, B15 &
B16 - The NE
4-6-0's

Vol.22
Class B1
(B18) to B9 -
The GCR
4-6-0's

Vol.26
Class J31 to
J37 - The
NBR 0-6-0's

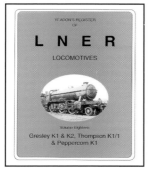

Vol.18
Gresley K1 &
K2,
Thompson
K1/1 and
Peppercorn
K1

Vol.23
Q5, Q6, Q7 &
Q10 - The
NER 0-8-0's

Vol.27
Class N7
Tank Engines

Vol.19
Class D1 to
D4 & the
M&GN 4-4-
0's

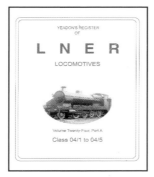

Vol.24A
Class O4
Parts 1 to 5

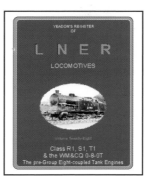

Vol.28
R1, S1, T1 &
the WM&CQ
0-8-0 - The
Pre-Group
Eight-
Coupled
tanks.

Vol.20
Class Q1 to
Q4 & the Q1
Tank Engines

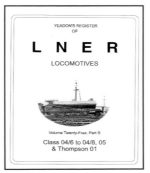

Vol.24B
Class O4
Parts 6 to 8,
O5 & the
Thompson O1

Vol.29
Class D5 to
D12 - the
GCR 4-4-0's

YEADON'S REGISTER

of

L N E R

LOCOMOTIVES

Volume Twenty- Five

Class N 1 & N 2

Copyright Booklaw/Railbus 2002
ISBN 1 899624 58 9

YEADON'S REGISTER OF L.N.E.R. LOCOMOTIVES - VOLUME 25

EDITOR'S NOTE & ACKNOWLEDGEMENTS

After the marathon of Volume 24 it is nice to once again return to a reasonable sized volume and herein is presented classes N1 and N2 making up the contents of Volume 25.

Both of these 0-6-2 tank types were products of the Great Northern Railway and though both were similar in outline they came from the drawing boards of two different Locomotive Engineers - H.A. Ivatt and H.N. Gresley.

Both classes had initially been designed to take care of the growing suburban traffic in London which the GNR had experienced during the first two decades of the twentieth century. Ivatt's N1 class had coped admirably in the seven years leading up to the Great War but once that conflict was over, and Britain started to get back to some normality, the growth in outer suburban traffic continued where it had left off and more N1's or their like were needed. Nigel Gresley, after having looked at a number of replacement designs, decided to enhance the Ivatt design with superheating, larger cylinders, piston valves, greater water capacity and many minor improvements. The result was the N2 class of which sixty entered LNER ownership to be followed in the period between 1925 and 1929 by forty-seven more similar engines. Some of this class also found work in Scotland besides the former GN lines.

The N1 and N2 classes enjoyed a long working lifespan and were still in employment when diesel traction began to take over much of their remaining duties. Though most of the N1's were withdrawn in the 1950's, the N2's lasted a little bit longer and it is perhaps one of the reasons why one of that class, No.69523, was purchased from British Railways by the Gresley Society for preservation. That particular feat has now been carried out and the engine is restored once again to working order. So, another happy ending for one particular class.

Eric Fry continues to toil through the thousands of numbers, letters and facts which make up each volume of the Register, checking everything with his careful eye for the errors which creep in during setting. Luckily his enthusiasm for the series, like his imput, is unwaving.

Brian Dyson and his staff continue to serve our every request for documents from the Archive at Hull University; Helen in particular seems to have the staying power when all the others move on after a short time.

Mike and Tina share the toil of typesetting and get our grateful thanks for doing so.

Annie, Jean and Simon continue to support the series and receive our blessing for doing so.

The next *Yeadon's Register of LNER Locomotives*, Volume 26, will feature the North British Railway's 0-6-0 tender engines of LNER classes J31 to J37.

The Yeadon Collection is available for inspection and anyone who wishes to
inspect it should contact:-
The Archivist
Brynmor Jones Library
University of Hull
Hull
HU6 7RX
Tel: 01482-465265
A catalogue of the Yeadon collection is available.

First published in the United Kingdom by
BOOKLAW/RAILBUS 2002 in association with CHALLENGER
382 Carlton Hill, Nottingham, NG4 1JA.
Printed and bound by The Amadeus Press, Cleckheaton, West Yorkshire.

INTRODUCTION

N1

In March 1907 Ivatt introduced an inside cylinder 0-6-2T design for use on the Great Northern's King's Cross suburban services, including the Metropolitan Widened Lines. This engine was built to replace Ivatt's earlier 0-8-2 tank engine (*see* Volume 28) which was found to be totally unsuitable for working in London. The 0-6-2T design, classified N1 by the GNR and given the running number 190, did not have a very good start to its intended career as it too was found to be rather heavy, especially at the leading coupled wheels and after just a few months it was sent away for further work in the West Riding.

A redistribution of weight was required and the design was altered (No.190 remained virtually as built) so that the rear of the frames were lengthened enabling the radial wheels to be placed further back. This in turn enabled a larger bunker to be built and with more space for water it was possible to shorten the side tanks without losing the original capacity. This newer design appeared later in the year and was straight away accepted, ten engines (Nos.1551 to 1560) coming out from Doncaster during the four month period from November 1907 to February 1908. Between February 1910 and June 1912 the Great Northern built a further forty-five of these Class N1 (LNER N1) 0-6-2 tank engines, all at Doncaster. These appeared in three batches of ten each and one of fifteen engines. Engine Order No.261 contained Nos.1561 to 1570; E.O. 264 Nos.1571 to 1580; E.O. 267 Nos.1581 to 1595; E.O. 268 Nos.1596 to 1605.

Except for Nos.1592 to 1595, each engine, including No.190, was provided at building with condensing apparatus so that they could work in the tunnels of the Metropolitan lines. In 1921 Nos.1554, 1556, 1560, 1564, 1566, 1568, 1569, 1572 and 1574 had their condensing gear removed as they were destined to work in the West Riding area where the apparatus was not required. No.190 which had been in Yorkshire from 1907 to 1921 had kept its condensing gear throughout the GN period and this was not removed until 1927 after it had undergone a six year stint at Hatfield shed prior to returning to Yorkshire. Further reallocations to the West Riding saw four more N1's losing their condensing gear in 1929 and in the 1930's more N1's were sent north losing their gear as a result. However, it was not all one-way traffic as two engines left Yorkshire during that decade going to London sheds and being fitted with condensing gear: No.4595, one of the original West Riding engines was fitted for the first time and sent south in 1931 whilst No.4554 was refitted in 1935 prior to its return to London. During WW2 another batch of N1's were sent to the West Riding and seven of them lost the condensing apparatus. Although it is by no means certain, some twenty N1's lost their condensing gear after transfer to West Riding sheds in LNER days.

None were superheated when built but from 1918 up to 1928, eleven of the class were superheated though these engines did retain their slide valves. The first of the class to get superheating was No.1598 which in February 1918 was fitted with the Schmidt superheater which had been disused since it was removed from J6 No.542 in 1913. The next N1 superheated was not dealt with until the eve of Grouping when No.1557 received another Schmidt type superheater in December 1922. The other nine engines were fitted with Robinson superheaters by the LNER, six in 1924 (4555, 4556, 4559, 4584, 4602 and

4603), off these No.4556 got a second-hand boiler whilst the others all got new boilers. No.4572 was superheated in 1925 and the last two, Nos.4592 and 4599 in 1928. The two Schmidt fitted engines were refitted with Robinson superheater as follows: 4557 in August 1932 and 4598 in May 1930. The superheated boiler used on the N1's was also standard during LNER days with classes D1, D2, J2, J5, J6 and N2.

Other than superheating and the removal of condensing apparatus, the N1's, changed little from their original appearance except for minor details. Ross 'pop' safety valves began to replace the Ramsbottom valves from March 1927 onwards when No.4577 was so fitted. Eventually the whole class received these safety valves. Many of those engines stationed in London Area were fitted with trip cock gear for working the Metropolitan lines from 1925 onwards.

Vacuum brakes were fitted throughout the class but two engines, Nos.1581 and 1582, were fitted with Westinghouse brake pumps in October 1921 for testing ECJS carriages. Though removed by November 1948, No.4582 was noted still fitted with the pump in December 1944. No.4581 probably kept its pump until September 1947.

During WW1, two N1's, Nos. 1587 and 1590, were sold to the War Office for operating armoured gun trains on sections of the East Coast. They were fitted out with armour plating and were still so clad when they were bought back from the Government in 1923 albeit by the LNER. This purchase brought the class once again to its original total of fifty-six engines.

During GNR days the standard livery for the class was green paint. Economy measures in 1912 saw at least two of the class, 1580 and 1584, painted in slate grey. The LNER kept the green livery at first but soon black with red lining became standard for the class. The lining disappeared during wartime but BR introduced the red, cream and grey lining for mixed traffic engines and so the N1's once again enjoyed full lining over their black paint - at least some of them did anyway. Up to September 1950, Doncaster had lined ten of the class before maintenance of the N1's was switched to Stratford works which normally did not line the engines after a repaint. All except the last two N1's repaired at Stratford (all the class managed at least one visit there) got plain black livery, the last two were in fact lined after their Stratford repairs in January and February 1954 at which time Doncaster once again became responsible for the class but they only put lining on two further engines.

The LNER renumbered the class 9430 to 9485. All except 9438 entered BR service though 9480 did not gain the 60000 addition to its number before it was withdrawn in June 1951.

Although normally shopped at Doncaster, Stratford has been responsible for part or all of the class from time to time. London area engines started going to Stratford in 1936 and this continued until 1939. Again during periods of WW2 some of the London engines went to Stratford for overhauls. As mentioned above the whole class were shopped at Stratford between September 1950 and February 1954 when Doncaster once again took over maintenance.

Besides their work on the inner suburban passenger trains in the London area and empty stock working, the class was also involved with the cross-London goods interchange traffic to South London via the Widened Lines. By the time the class had been completed in 1912, King's Cross and Hornsey sheds had

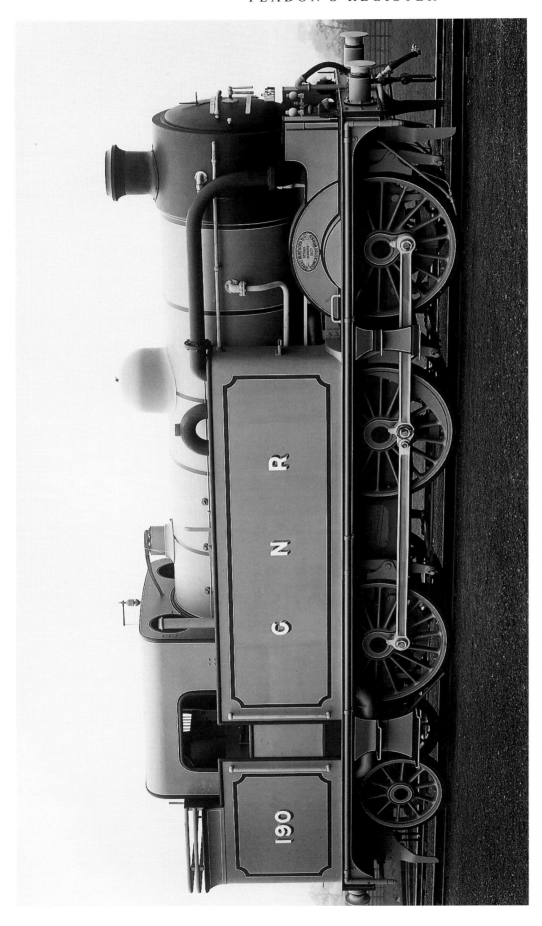

The first engine of what was to become LNER Class N1, was built by the Great Northern Railway at Doncaster in March 1907. This sole example, No.190, was fitted with condensing apparatus to work the London District suburban traffic. Note the short cover for the Ramsbottom safety valves, and the clack box on the front ring of the boiler, which was second-hand from D2 Class, having being built for No.1322 in 1898 and also used on No.1372.

fifty N1's between them the majority at the former shed, five were in the West Riding at Copley Hill and Bradford and one solitary example resided at Hatfield. When Gresley introduced the N2 class in 1920 the N1's handed over much of the inner suburban work to the newer engines and by Grouping their numbers had dwindled in London with thirteen of the class now stationed in the West Riding, split between Ardsley and Bradford sheds. This situation remained virtually unchanged until the early 1940's when ten of the London based N1's were exchanged for ten West Riding based N2's. Prior to WW2 a couple of N1's were allocated to Colwick for working Nottingham (Victoria) - Mansfield local passenger trains, however, these two did not stay long on those duties and went next to Woodford for a short period before returning to London in 1941. When BR came into being, the number of N1's in Yorkshire had risen to twenty-four and eventually this rose to thirty as Hornsey engines were relegated from London area work in the early 1950's. These London area N1's, still with condensing gear went to the West Riding with the gear fitted but it was blanked off at the sheds prior to, in most cases, a complete removal at works.

In 1954 nine of the Hornsey based N1's went to Colwick to work local services including Derby to Nottingham for which a couple were shedded at Friargate shed.

By now the class was still fairly intact but inroads by the scrapman were being made. The first withdrawal had been made by the LNER in February 1947 when No.9438 was condemned. Another one had succumbed in 1951 and then a couple more in 1952 with three in 1953. The following year saw eight of the class condemned one of which, No.69461 withdrawn in June, was sent as a stationary boiler on carriage heating duties to Shoeburyness where it worked from November 1954 until December 1962 - technically the last N1. 1955 proved to be the point of no return for the class when no less than twenty N1's were condemned. At the start of 1956 Hornsey shed had just three left with the other eighteen survivors dispersed amongst the three West Riding sheds; in August the last of the Hornsey N1's was withdrawn ending nearly fifty continuous years of N1 residence. Copley Hill shed had the distinction of withdrawing the last N1, 69462 in April 1959.

N2

The need for more passenger tank engines on the Great Northern came about shortly after the cessation of the First World War and in 1919 Gresley drew up plans for an improved version of Ivatt's Class N1 0-6-2T. Two other designs were also considered comprising a 2-6-2T and a 2-6-4T; the former wheelbase would materialise later in the LNER period in the form of the Gresley's Class V1 and V3 tanks and the latter wheelbase would appear at the end of the LNER period in the shape of Thompson's L1 tanks (see Volume 16). In the meantime Gresley's improved N1 design, classified N2, had a very similar outline to its predecessor but there were a number of subtle differences. The most noticeable was probably the higher pitch of the boiler which was brought about because piston valves were fitted above the larger diameter inside cylinders. In order to allow the N2 access to the Metropolitan lines the boiler fittings were squatter than those on the N1's, although engines intended for working elsewhere on the LNER had a somewhat taller chimney. The side tanks were also longer reaching forward to the front of the middle pair of coupled wheels much like the original N1, No.190. The whole class was superheated from new and Wakefield mechanical lubricators were fitted for cylinder lubrication.

Sixty N2's were built by the GNR, Nos.4606 to 4615 and 4721 to 4770, these all having condensing gear, short chimney, and right-hand drive. From 1928 onwards the LNER designated these engines Class N2 Part 1. Of this GN batch, ten were built at Doncaster and fifty in Glasgow by the North British Locomotive Co. All were in service by August 1921.

From 1925 to 1929 the LNER added a further forty-seven N2's to the fleet. All these engines differed from the GN engines in having left-hand drive but there were other differences also and three more class Parts were created. The eighteen built in 1925, for instance, did not have condensing gear fitted when new, all had tall chimneys but Nos.892 to 897, built at Doncaster, had larger axlebox journals than the Nos.2583 to 2594 batch built by Beyer, Peacock & Co., Gorton. The latter became Part 2 and the Doncaster built engines became Part 3.

During the period between September 1928 and April 1929 the final twenty-nine N2's were built, Hawthorn Leslie & Co. supplying Nos.2662 to 2681, and Yorkshire Engine Co. Nos.2682 to 2690. All of these contractor built engines were fitted with condenser gear except the last six of the Yorkshire Engine Co. batch; these six became Part 3 engines whilst the other became Part 4. Some of the contractor built engines not fitted with condensing gear when new were fitted with it in the early 1930's.

No.4737 went, on loan, to the Scottish Area in April 1924 and began working the Glasgow (Queen Street) to Helensburgh service in addition to local work in the area. In August it returned to King's Cross. Following these trials, new N2's Nos.892 to 897 and 2583 to 2594 were delivered to the Scottish Area in 1925. They were joined from August 1927 by Nos.4721 to 4740, released from King's Cross. Finally, new engines Nos.2685 to 2690 arrived by early 1929 making a total of forty-four N2's in Scotland. They were employed mostly on duties around Edinburgh, Glasgow and Dundee. At that time the rest of the class were in the King's Cross district, with fifty-seven at that shed and six at Hornsey.

The N2's did not prove to be successful in Scotland - in particular they were unkind to the track with and derailments, followed by speed restrictions, resulted. Gresley's 2-6-2T design Class V1 was introduced in September 1930 and was better suited to the needs of the Scottish Area (see also Volume 16). Nos.2900 to 2927 were delivered during 1930-31 and enabled a like number of N2's to be permanently transferred to the Southern Area, some to the G.E. Section. This left sixteen in Scotland which remained, mostly allocated to Parkhead and Kipps sheds, until eventual withdrawal during 1957-61. However, Nos.4729, 4731 and 4732 were briefly on loan to Stratford during 1941.

Trials took place from Gateshead shed with Nos.893, 2689 and 2690 during 1931-33, but the NE Area found that the N2's did not meet their requirements. Apart from No.4739 working from Heaton for two years from July 1934 and a four-month stay by No.4724 allocated to Darlington in January 1942 (actually shedded at Northallerton where it clocked up 1782 working miles), no further use was made of the class in the NE Area.

Twelve of the 4721 to 4740 batch, sent to Scotland in 1927-28, were given Westinghouse pumps for alternative train braking, keeping their vacuum for the engine brake. Nos.4728, 4732 and 4735 were done at Doncaster prior to despatch and Nos.4721 to 4724, 4726, 4729, 4731, 4737 and 4740 at Cowlairs. The pumps were eventually removed, those from 4722, 4723, 4726, 4737 and 4740 at Stratford after they were sent south again and the rest at Cowlairs but this was a slow process and took place between 1939 and the end of the LNER. Six others, Nos.892 to

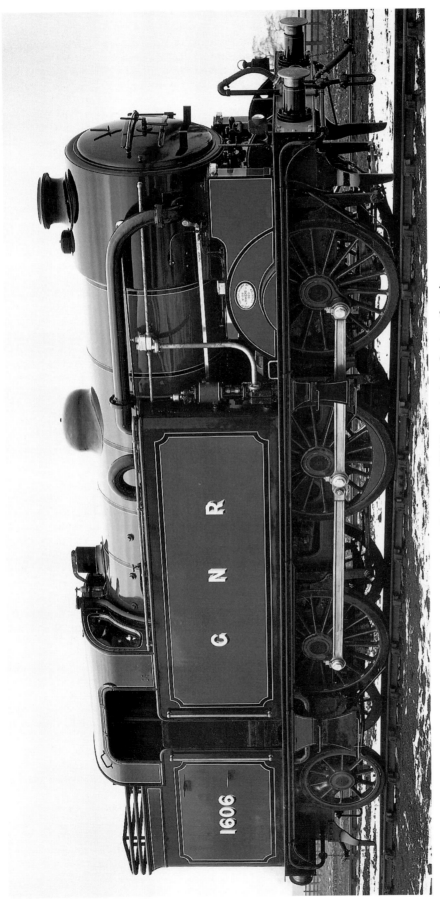

One engine, No.1606 was built at Doncaster in December 1920 and from April to August 1921 Doncaster turned out another nine of the same class, Nos.1607 to 1615. These ten were to form the first lot of LNER Class N2. Only No.1606 had the extra two rails at the back of the bunker and these were quickly taken off by King's Cross shed.

897, were built with Westinghouse pumps for the engine and train braking, plus vacuum for alternative train braking. When these too lost the Westinghouse gear, they received steam brake for the engine, plus VE in the case of 892 to 895, done at Cowlairs in the period between 1949 and 1955. Nos.896 and 897 however had gone south and they were converted at Stratford in 1938 but received vacuum for both engine and train. So, the brake progression was:-

4721, 4722, 4723, 4724, 4726, 4728, 4729, 4731, 4732, 4735, 4737, 4740 V, V+W, back to V.
892, 893, 894, 895 W+V, to S+V.
896, 897 W+V, to V.

All of the 4721 to 4740 batch sent to Scotland had their condensing gear removed during 1927-28. Five had it reinstated permanently in 1931-32 when they returned south and one, No.4730, had it removed again just a month after it had been refitted in October 1932 (this engine went back to Scotland then). Of the engines built without condensing gear, Nos.2588 and 2589 were fitted with it during 1932 (though it was removed from No.2588 about 1942) and Nos.2685, 2686 and 2687 gained the gear in 1931-32.

Some of the engines received from Hawthorn Leslie in 1928-29, Nos.2662 to 2681, went to Doncaster works for light repairs shortly after their delivery to the LNER. Therefore, it will be noted that the 'To traffic' dates are in fact prior to their short visit to Doncaster and they may not have been accepted into traffic until after release from Doncaster, which in turn casts doubt over the 'To traffic' date heading the table. To cast further doubt on Nos.2662 to 2681's entry into traffic, Nos.2682 to 2684, delivered from Yorkshire Engine Co., had Light repairs at Doncaster and were then allocated to the Southern Area and therefore 'To traffic' on the day of release from Doncaster. To add further interest, Nos.2685 to 2690 which were destined for Scottish Area, were delivered to Doncaster works from the same contractor and checks (Light repairs) were again promptly carried out but the 'To traffic' date was counted as the date the engine was allocated to Scotland; usually this date was a week or more after release from Doncaster works. To round off this particular episode of contractor supplied engines, it will be noted in the tables that Cowlairs duly checked over each engine on arrival in Scotland.

Apart from the former GN and GE lines in the London

area having their fair share, there were also useful numbers in the West Riding. The Yorkshire based engines had left the district by the end of WW2, some to London whilst a handful went to Colwick. This situation remained virtually unchanged throughout the BR period except for the final years of steam working around King's Cross when a number went to New England and Grantham mainly for want of work.

Three works in England maintained the N2's, Doncaster and Stratford throughout most of their lives but Gorton also did a number of general overhauls on Southern Area based engines during the mid-1930's. Cowlairs took care of the Scottish based N2's, with Inverurie repairing three in the mid-1950's.

Livery of the GN built engines comprised lined-out passenger green, however from the start of the LNER period the green gave way to black which was lined red until the WW2 economies saw the red lining dropped. One engine, No.9522, came out from a Doncaster repair in November 1946 fully lined-out and in apple green paint. This was to be the new livery for the class but in the event only this one engine was so treated and that reverted to the standard BR lined black in 1949.

The LNER renumbered this class 9490 to 9596 and all went on into BR service. In September 1955, No.69514 became the first N2 to be withdrawn but it was a one-off withdrawal and the class stayed intact until 1957 when scrapping began in earnest. 1962 was the last year that the N2's worked and the thirteen members of the class surviving into September of that year were withdrawn en masse though one of those, 69523, was preserved and is running today, owned and maintained by the Gresley Society as LNER 4744.

For easier access by the Gresley Society's members who maintain it, No.4744 was moved by low-loader on 27th November 1975 from Ingrow to Quorn and Woodhouse on the Great Central Railway. Since then, it has been housed at Loughborough and used for passenger workings. It has since appeared in BR livery (and with different numbers) and is currently being painted in GNR green livery.

The first ten engines of the production series, Nos.1551 to 1560, were built at Doncaster between the following November and February 1908. These had shorter tanks but that was compensated by a tank in the bunker, which was itself enlarged by making the frames 12 inches longer and placing the radial wheels 6 inches further to the rear.

From February to April 1910, Nos.1561 to 1570 were built at Doncaster, similar to the previous ten, and fitted also with condensing gear.

CLASS N 1

3190

Doncaster 1145.

To traffic 3/1907.

REPAIRS:
Don. ?/?—?/7/16.**G.**
Don. 6/7—12/12/21.**G.**
Re-painted green.
Don. 3/4—20/6/25.**G.**
Don. 27/5—20/8/27.**G.**
Condensing gear removed.
Don. 31/8—5/10/29.**G.**
Don. 25/7—22/8/31.**G.**
Don. 8—29/7/33.**G.**
Don. 24/10—14/11/36.**G.**
Don. 10—17/7/37.**L.**
Don. 15/4—13/5/39.**G.**
Don. 31/1—28/2/42.**G.**
Don. 15/7—5/8/44.**G.**
Don. 29/6—10/8/47.**G.**
Don. 10—30/3/49.**C/L.**
Str. 23/10—16/12/50.**G.**
Don. 20/7—21/8/51.**C/L.**
Str. 28/2—3/4/52.**C/L.**
Str. 27/10—15/11/52.**C/L.**
Don. 8/3—2/4/54.**G.**
Don. 17/6—7/7/55.**G.**

BOILERS:
1322.
6853 ?/7/16.
7758 20/6/25.
8709 29/7/33.
9493 5/8/44.
21476 16/12/50.
21471 2/4/54.

SHEDS:
Hatfield.
Ardsley 20/8/27.
Copley Hill 24/8/41.

RENUMBERED:
3190 20/6/25.
9430 10/11/46.
69430 30/3/49.

CONDEMNED: 10/12/56.
Cut up at Doncaster.

4551

Doncaster 1176.

To traffic 11/1907.

REPAIRS:
Don. ?/?—?/4/18.**G.**
Don. 8/10—11/12/20.**G.**
Don. 30/8—7/12/23.**G.**
Don. 26/4—21/8/26.**G.**
Don. 2/2—9/3/29.**G.**
Don. 18/5—1/6/29.**L.**
Don. 2—23/5/31.**G.**
Don. 19/8—23/9/33.**G.**
Don. 19/9—10/10/36.**G.**
Don. 17—31/8/40.**G.**
Don. 4—25/11/44.**G.**
Don. 4/2—10/3/48.**G.**
Str. 3/7—1/9/51.**G.**
Str. 18—19/9/51.**N/C.**
Str. 25/11/53—2/1/54.**C/L.**
Don. 22/2/55. *Not repaired.*

BOILERS:
6851.
6854 ?/4/18.
7407 9/3/29.
8389 31/8/40.
8537 10/3/48.
21490 1/9/51.

SHEDS:
Hornsey.
Ardsley 9/8/26.
King's Cross 23/5/31.
Hornsey 4/5/34.
Ardsley 22/3/53.

RENUMBERED:
1551N 7/12/23.
4551 21/8/26.
9431 17/11/46.
E**9431** 10/3/48.
69431 1/9/51.

CONDEMNED: 7/3/55.
Cut up at Doncaster.

4552

Doncaster 1177.

To traffic 12/1907.

REPAIRS:
Don. 26/3—19/6/20.**G.**
Don. 18/4—14/7/23.**G.**
In LNER black.
Don. 9/11/25—3/2/26.**G.**
Don. 1/6—6/7/29.**G.**
Don. 18/7—15/8/31.**G.**
Don. 2—9/4/32.**L.**
Don. 28/4—19/5/34.**G.**
Str. 5/3—9/4/38.**G.**
Don. 18/4—9/5/42.**G.**
Don. 13/10—10/11/45.**G.**
Don. 30/12/46—15/2/47.**G.**
Don. 6/3—2/4/49.**G.**
Str. 4/6—2/8/52.**G.**
Don. 31/12/53—4/2/54.**C/L.**
Don. 28/10/54. *Not repaired.*

BOILERS:
6852.
6869 19/6/20.
8412 15/8/31.
8705 9/4/38.
8392 2/4/49.
21515 2/8/52.

SHEDS:
Hornsey.
Ardsley 2/7/29.
King's Cross 18/8/31.
Hornsey 31/7/34.
Bradford 24/6/51.

RENUMBERED:
4552 3/2/26.
9432 13/9/46.
69432 2/4/49.

CONDEMNED: 8/11/54.
Cut up at Doncaster.

4553

Doncaster 1178.

To traffic 12/1907.

REPAIRS:
Don. ?/?—?/10/19.**G.**
Don. 31/5—14/10/22.**G.**
Kx. 17/11/23—15/3/24.**L.**
Wheels sent to Doncaster.
Don. 18/8—15/11/24.**G.**
Don. 14/4—23/7/27.**G.**
Don. 1/2—1/3/30.**G.**
Don. 23/9—21/10/33.**G.**
Str. 7/11/36—30/1/37.**G.**
Don. 28/6—26/7/41.**G.**
Don. 23/3—20/4/46.**G.**
Don. 6/7—13/8/48.**G.**
Don. 1—15/2/49.**C/L.**
Str. 8/11—19/12/51.**G.**
Don. 28/11/54. *Not repaired.*

BOILERS:
6850.
6851 ?/10/19.
7999 23/7/27.
8470 13/8/48.
21505 19/12/51.

SHEDS:
Hornsey.
Bradford 22/2/53.

RENUMBERED:
4553 15/11/24.
9433 17/11/46.
69433 13/8/48.

CONDEMNED: 27/12/54.
Cut up at Doncaster.

4554

Doncaster 1179.

To traffic 12/1907.

REPAIRS:
Don. ?/?—?/6/15.**G.**
Don. 27/10/20—12/3/21.**G.**
Don. 25/6—29/10/23.**G.**
Don. 13/3—23/6/26.**G.**
Don. 19/5—1/11/28.**G.**
Don. 10/1—14/2/31.**G.**
Don. 28/2—3/3/31.**N/C.**
Don. 4/3—1/4/33.**G.**
Don. 1—22/6/35.**G.**
Don. 30/8—20/9/35.**L.**
Don. 18/2—18/3/39.**G.**
Str. 31/8—10/10/42.**G.**
Don. 1—15/1/44.**G.**
Don. 17/6—16/8/47.**G.**
Don. 18/4—19/5/50.**G.**
Str. 26/10—6/12/52.**G.**

WORKS CODES:- Bpk - Beyer, Peacock. Cw - Cowlairs. Dar- Darlington. Don - Doncaster. Ghd - Gateshead. Gor - Gorton. Inv - Inverurie. Str - Stratford.
REPAIR CODES:- **C/H** - Casual Heavy. **C/L** - Casual Light. **G** - General. **H**- Heavy. **H/I** - Heavy Intermediate. **L** - Light. **L/I** - Light Intermediate. **N/C** - Non-Classified.

7

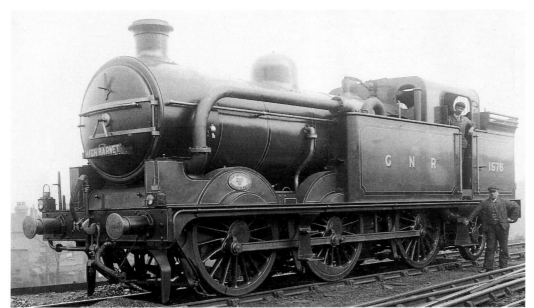

(left) Twenty-five engines, Nos.1571 to 1595 were built at Doncaster from November 1910 to April 1912 of which Nos.1571 to 1591 had condensing apparatus fitted, and were similar to the preceding batches.

(below) The last four of the order, Nos.1592 to 1595, were to work in the West Riding and so did not need to be fitted with condensing apparatus. They did however carry destination board brackets, used in London and Nottingham districts but not in the West Riding during the LNER period. Bradford shed, 7th July 1935.

A further batch of ten, Nos.1596 to 1605, was built at Doncaster from May to June 1912 and these too were fitted with condensing apparatus. Hitchin, 19th April 1949.

On 10th December 1914, No.1587, and then No.1590 on 31st March 1915, were sold to the War Office so that they could be used for hauling armoured gun trains as part of East Coast defences. Both were re-purchased, but not until 3rd March 1923, when they became LNER stock.

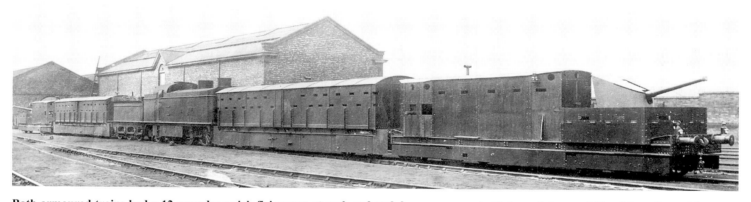

Both armoured trains had a 12-pounder quick firing gun at each end and, by vacuum controlled regulator, could be driven from either end. This is No.2 train which differed from No.1 train by the inclusion of a Stirling tender to provide extra water capacity. No.1 train was based on the M&GNR at North Walsham and ran on the Norfolk coastline. No.2 train was stationed at Edinburgh, mainly for Forth Bridge defence, although it did work up to Aberdeen.

(right) After the war, the engines were stored for a short while at Catterick, but by late 1919 were on the Woolmer Instructional Military Railway at Longmoor in Hampshire. Not until January 1923 did the Disposals Board offer them for sale and this illustration shows them on arrival at Doncaster on 3rd March 1923. No.587 was back to normal traffic on the 13th May and No.1590 followed on 4th June. No.1 train engine was named NORMA and No.2 was ALICE, but neither name was retained by the LNER.

4554 cont/.
Don. 3/3—5/4/55.**G.**
Don. 18/9—16/10/56.**C/L.**
Don. 5/3/59. *Not repaired.*

BOILERS:
6853.
6951 ?/6/15.
7004 1/11/28.
7755 14/2/31.
8470 1/4/33.
9805 16/8/47.
21475 6/12/52.
21355 5/4/55.

SHEDS:
Bradford.
Hitchin 12/1/24.
Ardsley 17/5/24.
Hatfield 16/2/31.
King's Cross 12/5/34.
Copley Hill 12/4/39.
King's Cross 6/3/41.
Hornsey 16/12/48.
Bradford 24/6/51.
Copley Hill 27/1/57.

RENUMBERED:
1554N 29/10/23.
4554 23/6/26.
9434 28/9/46.
69434 19/5/50.

CONDEMNED: 10/3/59.
Cut up at Doncaster.

4555

Doncaster 1180.

To traffic 12/1907.

REPAIRS:
Don. ?/?—?/4/15.**G.**
Don. 26/8—23/10/20.**G.**
Don. 6/12/23—14/4/24.**G.**
Don. 18/10/26—15/1/27.**G.**
Don. 23/11—21/12/29.**G.**
Don. 30/9—4/11/33.**G.**
Don. 1—29/8/36.**G.**
Don. 16/9—7/10/39.**G.**
Don. 12/2—11/3/44.**G.**
Don. 12/9—7/11/47.**G.**
Str. 13/3—28/4/51.**G.**
Don. 17/3/55. *Not repaired.*

BOILERS:
6854.
7058 ?/4/15.
7673 *(sup.)* 14/4/24.
8273 7/10/39.
21483 28/4/51.

SHED:
Hornsey.

RENUMBERED:
4555 14/4/24.
9435 24/11/46.
69435 28/4/51.

CONDEMNED: 21/3/55.
Cut up at Doncaster.

4556

Doncaster 1181.

To traffic 12/1907.

REPAIRS:
Don. 3/11/20—2/4/21.**G.**
Don. 2/4—23/8/24.**G.**
Don. 16/2—2/5/25.**L.**
Don. 27/10/26—14/1/27.**G.**
Don. 5/10—2/11/29.**G.**
Don. 26/3—7/5/32.**G.**
Don. 16—30/11/35.**G.**
Don. 9—23/10/37.**G.**
Don. 5/10—2/11/40.**G.**
Don. 8—29/11/41.**L.**
Don. 10—24/10/42.**G.**
Don. 8/12/45—5/1/46.**L.**
Don. 7—21/9/46.**L.**
Don. 1—31/1/49.**G.**
Str. 27/9—18/10/50.**C/L.**
Str. 4/1—24/2/51.**C/H.**
Str. 2—31/1/53.**G.**
Str. 1—5/3/53.**C/L.**
Don. 3/7/55. *Not repaired.*

BOILERS:
6865.
7214 *(sup.)* 23/8/24.
8543 7/5/32.
9059 23/10/37.
8996 31/1/49.
8996 reno.21480 24/2/51.
21473 31/1/53.

SHEDS:
Copley Hill.
Bradford 15/8/54.

RENUMBERED:
4556 23/8/24.
9436 20/10/46.
69436 29/1/49.

CONDEMNED: 11/7/55.
Cut up at Doncaster.

4557

Doncaster 1182.

To traffic 12/1907.

REPAIRS:
Don. 5/7—4/12/22.**G.**
Don. 6/3—23/5/25.**G.**
Don. 17/9—18/11/27.**G.**
Don. 26/10—16/11/29.**G.**
Don. 2/7—6/8/32.**G.**
Don. 20/4—11/5/35.**G.**
Fountain lub.
Don. 27/3—17/4/37.**G.**
Don. 27/4—25/5/40.**G.**
Don. 26/2—11/3/44.**G.**
Don. 10—24/3/45.**L.**
Don. 8/6—13/7/46.**G.**
Don. 1/10—16/11/48.**G.**
Str. 14/9—27/10/51.**G.**
Don. 23/1—20/2/52.**C/L.**
Don. 13/7/54. *Not repaired.*

BOILERS:
6866.
7240 *(sup.)* 4/12/22.
D1756 (exJ6 3521) 6/8/32.
8276 25/5/40.
1362 13/7/46.
21502 27/10/51.

SHEDS:
Hornsey.
Bradford 3/12/42.
Ardsley 18/4/48.
Copley Hill 5/12/48.

RENUMBERED:
4557 23/5/25.
9437 24/11/46.
69437 16/11/48.

CONDEMNED: 19/7/54.
Cut up at Doncaster.

4558

Doncaster 1183.

To traffic 2/1908.

REPAIRS:
Don. 10/4—5/6/20.**G.**
Don. 11/4—22/8/23.**G.**
*LNER lined black livery with
original number.*
Don. 16/1—20/2/26.**G.**
Don. 20/7—24/8/29.**G.**
Don. 27/5—17/6/33.**G.**
Don. 7—21/12/35.**G.**
Don. 1—29/7/39.**G.**
Don. 27/4—8/6/40.**G.**
Don. 16/10—13/11/43.**G.**
Don. 19/11/46—17/2/47.
Not repaired.

BOILERS:
6867.
6850 5/6/20.
7075 20/2/26.
8877 21/12/35.

SHEDS:
Hornsey.
Bradford 5/4/46.

RENUMBERED:
4558 12/3/25.
9438 29/9/46.

CONDEMNED: 17/2/47.
Cut up at Doncaster.

4559

Doncaster 1184.

To traffic 1/1908.

REPAIRS:
Don. 7/10—27/11/20.**G.**
Don. 29/11/23—15/3/24.**G.**
Don. 13/11/26—5/2/27.**G.**
Don. 13/4—25/5/29.**G.**
Don. 26/9—24/10/31.**G.**
Don. 9/12/33—20/1/34.**G.**
Str. 15/8—26/9/36.**G.**
Don. 22/7—2/9/39.**G.**
Str. 5/12/42—1/5/43.**G.**
Don. 4/12/46—18/1/47.**G.**
Don. 15/5—20/6/50.**G.**
Str. 2/12/52—10/1/53.**G.**
Str. 20/1/53.**N/C.**

BOILERS:
6868.
7675 *(sup.)* 15/3/24.
8714 20/1/34.
9062 20/6/50.
21524 10/1/53.

SHEDS:
Hornsey.
Bradford 24/6/51.

RENUMBERED:
4559 15/3/24.
9439 26/1/46.
69439 20/6/50.

CONDEMNED: 11/11/55.
Cut up at Doncaster.

This class was also directly affected by the Second World War. Nos.4573 and 4575 suffered damage by splinters from a land mine at Harringay on 26th September 1940. Note the GNR shed allocation plate was still carried at the rear of the cab roof although it had ceased to have effect from 1924, some sixteen years earlier.

The odd boiler with the short safety valves put on No.190 was taken off in June 1916 and then stood spare until carried by No.1589 from 7th February 1920 to 31st March 1925, after which it was cut up.

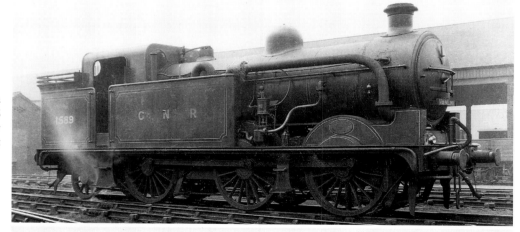

On No.3190, the apron plate giving access to the slide valves was vertical and had a pocket to cover the valve tail rods.

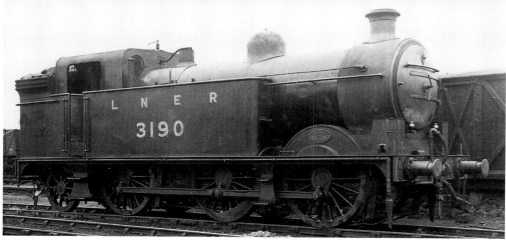

(left) **All the other fifty-five engines had an apron plate shaped to match the contour of the frame end; two knobs were fitted to secure. Bradford shed.**

(below) **Originally, the knobs on Nos.4581 to 4605 were nearer the top of the apron plate to give better leverage but much changing took place. King's Cross, April 1936.**

On new boilers from 1934, and where a new firebox casing was fitted, inspection covers were put on instead of the washout plugs. To 1911 the dome height was 2ft 2in. and 1ft 11¼in. thereafter, but all dome covers were the same height and style. Copley Hill, 6th July 1947.

4560

Doncaster 1185.

To traffic 2/1908.

REPAIRS:
Don. ?/?—?/3/18.**G.**
Don. 7/10/20—5/3/21.**G.**
Don. 16/7—29/10/23.**G.**
Don. 8/12/25—12/3/26.**G.**
Don. 12/11/27—6/1/28.**G.**
Don. 31/5—5/7/30.**G.**
Don. 31/3—21/4/34.**G.**
Don. 29/8—26/9/36.**G.**
Don. 16—23/7/38.**G.**
Don. 4—25/1/41.**G.**
Don. 4—25/9/43.**G.**
Don. 30/9—7/10/44.**L.**
Don. 3/11—14/12/46.**G.**
Don. 20/12/47—12/1/48.**L.**
Don. 4/1—17/2/50.**G.**
Str. 24/1—1/3/52.**C/H.**
Str. 20/7—15/8/52.**C/L.**
Str. 2/10—7/11/53.**G.**
Don. 7/3/57. *Not repaired.*

BOILERS:
6869.
7144 ?/3/18.
7053 6/1/28.
7758 21/4/34.
8191 23/7/38.
9491 14/12/46.
9491 reno.21510 1/3/52.
21527 7/11/53.

SHEDS:
Bradford.
Hatfield 6/1/24.
Bradford 30/6/24.
Copley Hill 2/2/31.
Bradford 1/3/41.
Copley Hill 1/4/41.
Ardsley 28/11/54.

RENUMBERED:
1560N 29/10/23.
4560 12/3/26.
9440 22/9/46.
69440 18/2/50.

CONDEMNED: 18/3/57.
Cut up at Doncaster.

4561

Doncaster 1256.

To traffic 2/1910.

REPAIRS:
Don. 16/4—10/7/20.**G.**
Don. 30/5—22/9/23.**G.**
Don. 8/2—19/6/26.**G.**
Don. 15/6—13/7/29.**G.**
Don. 2—30/7/32.**G.**
Don. 17/11—1/12/34.**G.**
Fountain lub. to horncheeks.
Str. 23/7—26/9/38.**G.**
Str. 26/9—20/12/42.**G.**
Str. 20/4—25/5/46.**G.**
Don. 31/5—6/7/49.**G.**
Str. 23/3—10/4/52.**C/L.**
Str. 6/10—13/11/52.**G.**

BOILERS:
6980.
6852 10/7/20.
6922 19/6/26.
8535 30/7/32.
8998 20/12/42.
9631 25/5/46.
21521 13/11/52.

SHEDS:
Hornsey.
Hatfield 25/12/38.
Hornsey 28/2/40.
Colwick 21/3/54.
Bradford 10/4/55.

RENUMBERED:
1561N 22/9/23.
4561 19/6/26.
9441 13/9/46.
69441 6/7/49.

CONDEMNED: 30/5/55.
Cut up at Doncaster.

4562

Doncaster 1257.

To traffic 3/1910.

REPAIRS:
Don. 26/4—16/7/21.**G.**
Don. 31/5—23/8/24.**G.**
Don. 30/4—27/7/27.**G.**
Don. 4/1—8/2/30.**G.**
Don. 18/2—25/3/33.**G.**
Rail washing gear fitted.
Don. 16/11—7/12/35.**G.**
Str. 8/5—21/6/39.**G.**
Don. 16/10—6/11/43.**G.**
Don. 4/5—14/6/47.**G.**
Str. 13/6—19/7/50.**C/L.**
Str. 14/1—3/3/51.**G.**
Don. 24/8/53. *Not repaired.*

BOILERS:
6981.
6980 16/7/21.
8468 25/3/33.
8734 21/6/39.
21478 3/3/51.

SHEDS:
Hornsey.
Bradford 30/11/52.

RENUMBERED:
4562 23/8/24.
9442 13/9/46.
69442 22/7/50.

CONDEMNED: 6/9/53.
Cut up at Doncaster.

4563

Doncaster 1258.

To traffic 2/1910.

REPAIRS:
Don. 23/11/21—11/3/22.**G.**
Don. 27/10/24—10/1/25.**G.**
Don. 15/8—5/11/27.**G.**
Don. 5/10—2/11/29.**G.**
Don. 10/10—7/11/31.**G.**
Don. 12—16/1/35.**G.**
Fountain lub to horncheeks.
Don. 8/5—5/6/37.**G.**
Don. 23/12/39—20/1/40.**G.**
Don. 29/8—12/9/42.**G.**
Don. 3/2—10/3/45.**G.**
Don. 19/10—2/11/46.**G.**
Don. 16/3—19/4/49.**G.**
Str. 6/5—28/7/51.**G.**
Str. 11/9—24/10/53.**G.**
Str. 9—11/11/53.**N/C.**
Don. 7/3—19/4/56.**G.**
Don. 7—27/3/57.**C/H.**
Don. 5/3/59. *Not repaired.*

BOILERS:
6983.
7645 11/3/22.
8729 26/1/35.
8388 12/9/42.
9146 2/11/46.
21487 28/7/51.
21485 24/10/53.
21356 19/4/56.
21493 27/3/57.

SHEDS:
King's Cross.
Ardsley 5/11/27.
Copley Hill 15/2/32.
Ardsley 25/5/32.
Bradford 3/1/42.
Ardsley 17/11/57.

RENUMBERED:
4563 10/1/25.
9443 22/9/46.
69443 19/4/49.

CONDEMNED: 11/3/59.
Cut up at Doncaster.

4564

Doncaster 1259.

To traffic 3/1910.

REPAIRS:
Don. 21/6—9/7/21.**G.**
Don. 2/7—13/10/23.**G.**
Don. 4/11/25—3/2/26.**G.**
Don. 12/7—19/9/28.**G.**
Don. 16/8—27/9/30.**G.**
Don. 5/9—17/10/31.**G.**
Don. 2—30/6/34.**G.**
Don. 23/1—13/2/37.**G.**
Fountain lub. to axleboxes.
Don. 29/4—27/5/39.**G.**
Don. 20/9—18/10/41.**G.**
Don. 12/2—4/3/44.**G.**
Don. 17/8—10/11/46.**G.**
Don. 20/2—21/4/50.**G.**
Don. 18/9—5/10/51.**C/L.**
Str. 6/3—11/4/53.**G.**

BOILERS:
6984.
6867 9/7/21.
8391 27/9/30.
8393 27/5/39.
9203 21/4/50.
21525 11/4/53.

SHEDS:
Bradford.
Hatfield 6/1/24.
Bradford 30/6/24.
Copley Hill 27/3/41.

RENUMBERED:
1564N 13/10/23.
4564 3/2/26.
9444 10/11/46.
69444 21/4/50.

CONDEMNED: 22/10/56.
Cut up at Doncaster.

4565

Doncaster 1260.

To traffic 3/1910.

REPAIRS:
Don. 12/12/22—7/4/23.**G.**
Lined black, lettered L&NER.
Don. 6/10/25—16/1/26.**G.**
Don. 30/8—30/10/28.**G.**
Don. 4/6—9/7/32.**G.**
Don. 25/5—8/6/35.**G.**

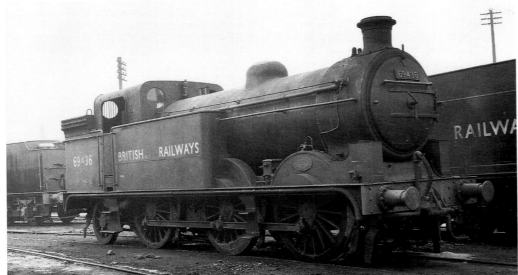

On boilers built from 1932 the dome height was cut to 1ft 4³/₄in. so as to interchange with N2 class, but on only a few N1 was a corresponding dome cover seen: No.69436 from 31st January 1949; 69465 probably from 19th January 1952; and 69470 possibly from a 16th February 1952 shopping.

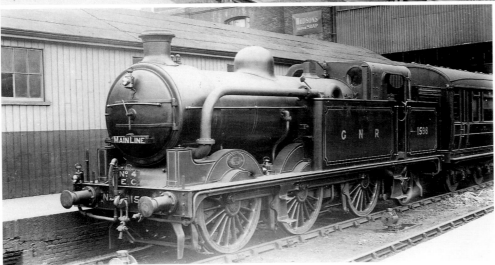

(above) No.4558 had its final repair in November 1943 and got this unusual flat top dome cover, the only one so noted. This photograph was taken 25th September 1946 and No.4558 was re-numbered 9438 on 29th September. It went to works 19th November but was not repaired, being withdrawn 17th February 1947 so LNER was not restored to it. Bradford Exchange, 25th September 1946.

(left) Ex-works 23rd February 1918, No.1598 had been fitted with a Schmidt superheated boiler from J6 class, and on 4th December 1922 No.1557 was out similarly fitted. Only these two had a superheater at Grouping; both were shedded at Hornsey. King's Cross station.

Nine others, Nos.4555, 4556, 4559, 4572, 4584, 4592, 4599, 4602 and 4603, were fitted with a superheater from 23rd February 1924 (4603) to 2nd June 1928 (4599) but of the Robinson type to which the two earlier ones were changed later, 4557 (6th August 1932) and 4598 (10th May 1930). To accommodate the header the chimney was moved forward. Curiously, all had, and kept, twin 'pepper-pot' anti-vacuum valves, and not the Gresley type. Doncaster, 20th June 1931.

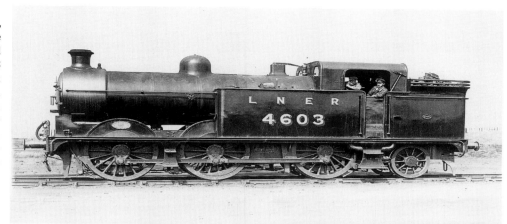

Engines which worked in the West Riding did not need condensing gear and No.3190, ex-works 20th August 1927 had it removed because it went to Ardsley instead of back to Hatfield shed. Doncaster shed.

There was only one which got the reverse process. No.4595 (9475 from 17th March 1946) did not have condensing gear until 15th August 1931 when ex-works so fitted on transfer from Bradford to Hornsey shed. Harringay.

When new, Nos.3190 and 4551 to 4570 had an air valve on the U-bend to prevent water surging to the cylinders.

4565 cont./
Don. 17/6—8/7/39.**G.**
Don. 26/2—18/3/44.**G.**
Don. 10—24/3/45.**L.**
Don. 8/4—27/5/47.**G.**
Str. 30/1—17/3/51.**G.**
Don. 31/3—13/4/54.**C/L.**
Don. 1/1/55. *Not repaired.*

BOILERS:
6982.
6866 7/4/23.
8533 9/7/32.
9802 27/5/47.
21479 17/3/51.

SHED:
Hornsey.

RENUMBERED:
4565 21/2/25.
9445 28/7/46.
69445 17/3/51.

CONDEMNED: 17/1/55.
Cut up at Doncaster.

4566

Doncaster 1261.

To traffic 3/1910.

REPAIRS:
Don. 27/10/20—9/4/21.**G.**
Don. 15/8—27/11/23.**G.**
Don. 1/7—30/10/26.**G.**
Don. 24/8—28/9/29.**G.**
Don. 12/12/31—16/1/32.**G.**
Don. 11—25/1/36.**G.**
Don. 25/12/37—8/1/38.**G.**
Don. 13/1—10/2/40.**G.**
Don. 2—30/1/43.**G.**
Don. 24/3—21/4/45.**G.**
Don. 1/2—5/3/48.**G.**
Don. 22/9—22/10/48.**L.**
Str. 16/4—23/6/51.**G.**
Don. 17/5/53. *Not repaired.*

BOILERS:
7000.
7405 28/9/29.
9004 8/1/38.
21485 23/6/51.

SHED:
Copley Hill.

RENUMBERED:
1566N 27/11/23.
4566 30/10/26.
9446 22/9/46.
E**9446** 5/3/48.
69446 22/10/48.

CONDEMNED: 15/6/53.
Cut up at Doncaster.

4567

Doncaster 1262.

To traffic 3/1910.

REPAIRS:
Don. 22/7—12/11/21.**G.**
Don. 10/12/23—8/3/24.**G.**
Don. 15/9—11/12/26.**G.**
Don. 13/4—22/5/29.**G.**
Don. 31/1—28/2/31.**G.**
Don. 14/1—11/2/33.**G.**
Don. 6—20/10/34.**G.**
Don. 25/7—22/8/36.**G.**
Str. 16/4—14/5/38.**G.**
Don. 26/10—23/11/40.**G.**
Str. 16/3—1/5/43.**G.**
Don. 3—24/6/44.**L.**
Don. 13/1—10/2/45.**G.**
Don. 2—27/11/46.**G.**
Don. 3—31/12/48.**G.**
Str. 5/4—26/5/51.**G.**
Don. 30/9—22/10/52.**C/L.**
Str. 30/11/53—16/1/54.**G.**

BOILERS:
7001.
7115 11/12/26.
8730 20/10/34.
8879 23/11/40.
8535 1/5/43.
8412 24/6/44.
21481 26/5/51.
21494 16/1/54.

SHEDS:
King's Cross.
Ardsley 5/12/26.
Hatfield 27/2/31.
Bradford 25/9/43.

RENUMBERED:
4567 8/3/24.
9447 27/10/46.
69447 31/12/48.

CONDEMNED: 26/10/56.
Cut up at Doncaster.

4568

Doncaster 1263.

To traffic 4/1910.

REPAIRS:
Don. 8/10/20—12/3/21.**G.**
Don. 16/8—8/12/23.**G.**
Don. 28/7—5/11/26.**G.**
Don. 13/8—16/10/29.**G.**
Don. 28/5—25/6/32.**G.**
Don. 3/8—7/9/35.**G.**
Don. 12/6—10/7/37.**G.**
Don. 8/7—5/8/39.**G.**
Don. 13/7—10/8/40.**L.**
Don. 7/3—4/4/42.**G.**
Don. 31/7—21/8/43.**L.**
Don. 15/1—5/2/44.**G.**
Don. 8/9—13/10/45.**G.**
Don. 14/12/47—23/1/48.**G.**
Don. 23/1—24/3/50.**G.**
Don. 8/12/50—10/1/51.**C/L.**
Str. 29/5—2/8/52.**G.**
Don. 8/12/52. *Not repaired.*

BOILERS:
7003.
6979 8/12/23.
8529 25/6/32.
9273 13/10/45.
8706 24/3/50.
21514 2/8/52.

SHEDS:
Bradford.
Ardsley 7/7/43.
Bradford 8/7/43.

RENUMBERED:
1568N 8/12/23.
4568 7/5/25.
9448 27/10/46.
E**9448** 23/1/48.
69448 24/3/50.

CONDEMNED: 12/1/53.
Cut up at Stratford.

4569

Doncaster 1264.

To traffic 4/1910.

REPAIRS:
Don. 7/10/20—5/3/21.**G.**
Don. 6/4—9/8/23.**G.**
Lettered LNER.
Don. 25/1—13/4/26.**G.**
Don. 12/3—30/6/28.**G.**
Don. 29/11—27/12/30.**G.**
Don. 23/7—20/8/32.**G.**
Don. 10/2—3/3/34.**G.**
Don. 5—19/12/36.**G.**
Fountain lub.
Don. 4—25/2/39.**G.**
Don. 9/3—6/4/40.**G.**
Str. 16/3—15/7/43.**G.**
Don. 9/2—16/3/46.**G.**
Don. 25/4—3/6/48.**G.**
Str. 17/7—2/9/50.**G.**
Str. 11/11—20/12/52.**G.**
Don. 3—30/6/54.**C/H.**

BOILERS:
7002.
7167 13/4/26.
8537 20/8/32.
9206 6/4/40.
8416 3/6/48.
9630 2/9/50.
9630 reno.21523 20/12/52.
21269 30/6/54.

SHEDS:
Bradford.
Hatfield 6/1/24.
Bradford 30/6/24.
Ardsley 26/3/41.
King's Cross 12/4/41.
Hatfield 27/4/41.
Bradford 7/1/44.

RENUMBERED:
4569 11/2/25.
9449 22/9/46.
69449 3/6/48.

CONDEMNED: 19/4/55.
Cut up at Doncaster.

4570

Doncaster 1265.

To traffic 4/1910.

REPAIRS:
Don. 27/9/22—26/2/23.**G.**
Green livery, lettered L&NER.
Don. 29/6—5/9/25.**G.**
Don. 17/3—19/9/28.**G.**
Don. 12/12/31—9/1/32.**G.**
Don. 15/12/34—12/1/35.**G.**
Fountain lub.
Str. 31/10—7/12/38.**G.**
Don. 17/7—7/8/43.**G.**
Don. 22/2—21/4/47.**G.**
Don. 5/11—16/12/49.**G.**
Str. 9/12/52—24/1/53.**G.**
Don. 29/7—18/9/53.**C/H.**
Don. 20/7—30/8/56.**G.**
Don. 14/8—17/10/57.**C/H.**
Don. 5/3/59. *Not repaired.*

BOILERS:
7004.
7412 19/9/28.
8002 7/12/38.
8705 16/12/49.
21493 24/1/53.
21210 30/8/56.

SHEDS:
King's Cross.
Hornsey 17/12/28.
Copley Hill 24/6/51.

Nos.4571 to 4580 had the same style U-bend casting but with the air valve blanked off. Nottingham Victoria.

Nos.4581 to 4605 had a plain casting for the U-bend, a drainpipe further forward having proved effective. Doncaster, April 1939.

When condensing apparatus was taken off, the vertical air vent pipe was usually removed, but at least nine, Nos.69430, 69434, 69450, 69453, 69457, 69461, 69479, 69482 and 69485, kept them to withdrawal.

The condenser-operating rod was low down on the right hand side and behind the wheel splashers.

When No.1598 was superheated the rod position had to be raised to clear the mechanical lubricator. King's Cross shed.

From September 1931 an improved operating arrangement led to the rod being placed above the splashers. Hornsey, July 1935.

Later still, an alteration to the leverage enabled the rod to be moved higher. Note the trip cock to the rear of the cab footstep; the normal position until 1950. Hornsey, July 1946.

4570 cont./
RENUMBERED:
4570 5/9/25.
9450 14/4/46.
69450 16/12/49.

CONDEMNED: 10/3/59.
Cut up at Doncaster.

4571

Doncaster 1286.

To traffic 11/1910.

REPAIRS:
Don. 18/10/22—5/4/23.**G.**
Lined black, lettered L&NER.
Don. 20/10/25—9/1/26.**G.**
Don. 21/12/27—10/3/28.**G.**
Don. 5/9—10/10/31.**G.**
Don. 16/3—6/4/35.**G.**
Fountain lub.
Str. 28/12/38—8/2/39.**G.**
Don. 7/12/40—4/1/41.**G.**
Air raid damage.
Don. 26/5—7/7/45.**G.**
Don. 29/11/47—23/1/48.**G.**
Str. 20/11/51—11/1/52.**G.**

BOILERS:
7016.
7108 9/1/26.
8416 10/10/31.
8700 8/2/39.
21506 11/1/52.

SHEDS:
Hornsey.
King's Cross 31/5/53.
Hornsey 5/7/53.
Colwick 3/1/54.
Bradford 10/4/55.

RENUMBERED:
4571 12/3/25.
9451 31/3/46.
ᴇ**9451** 23/1/48.
69451 11/1/52.

CONDEMNED: 12/10/55.
Cut up at Doncaster.

4572

Doncaster 1287.

To traffic 11/1910.

REPAIRS:
Don. 16/3—25/6/21.**G.**
Don. 7/11/24—21/2/25.**G.**
Don. 28/4—2/7/27.**G.**
Don. 16—23/2/29.**G.**
Don. 5/9—10/10/31.**G.**
Don. 7—28/10/33.**G.**
Don. 22/6—27/7/35.**G.**
Don. 23/10—6/11/37.**G.**
Don. 21/3—16/4/38.**L.**
Don. 8—22/6/40.**G.**
Don. 13/2—13/3/43.**G.**
Don. 12/5—16/6/45.**G.**
Don. 2/1—4/2/48.**G.**
Str. 30/11/50—6/1/51.**G.**
Str. 27/3—9/5/53.**G.**
Don. 5/3—13/4/56.**G.**

BOILERS:
7017.
7741 *(Sup.)* 21/2/25.
8713 28/10/33.
8833 27/7/35.
8108 16/6/45.
9058 4/2/48.
9058 reno.21477 6/1/51.
21480 9/5/53.
21386 13/4/56.

SHEDS:
Bradford.
Ardsley 8/4/41.

RENUMBERED:
4572 21/2/25.
9452 22/9/46.
ᴇ**9452** 4/2/48.
69452 6/1/51.

CONDEMNED: 13/3/59.
Into Don. for cut up 16/3/59.

4573

Doncaster 1288.

To traffic 12/1910.

REPAIRS:
Don. 3/6—8/10/21.**G.**
Don. 5/8—22/11/24.**G.**
Don. 4/8—9/11/27.**G.**
Don. 27/9—18/10/30.**G.**
Don. 22/12/33—20/1/34.**G.**
Str. 22/8—10/10/36.**G.**
Don. 9/11—7/12/40.**G.**
Don. 9/12/44—6/1/45.**G.**
Don. 9/5—22/6/48.**G.**
Str. 14/8—6/10/51.**G.**
Str. 2—27/11/53.**C/L.**

Don. 5/7—3/8/54.**C/H.**
Don. 26/1—16/2/55.**C/H.**
Don. 9/2—24/3/56.**G.**

BOILERS:
7018.
7107 9/11/27.
8337 10/10/36.
21498 6/10/51.
21353 16/2/55.

SHEDS:
Hornsey.
Colwick 18/4/54.
Ardsley 20/3/55.

RENUMBERED:
4573 22/11/24.
9453 28/9/46.
69453 19/6/48.

CONDEMNED: 29/4/58.
Cut up at Doncaster.

4574

Doncaster 1289.

To traffic 12/1910.

REPAIRS:
Don. 17/3—3/8/21.**G.**
Don. 18/5—19/9/25.**G.**
Don. 3/12/27—18/2/28.**G.**
Don. 21/6—10/8/28.**L.**
Don. 22/2—15/3/30.**G.**
Don. 11/3—8/4/33.**G.**
Don. 30/5—20/6/36.**G.**
Don. 13—27/8/38.**G.**
Don. 30/3—20/4/40.**G.**
Don. 13/7—1/8/42.**G.**
Don. 4—25/11/44.**G.**
Don. 31/8—28/9/46.**G.**
Don. 16/12/47—30/1/48.**G.**
Don. 14/12/49—20/1/50.**G.**
Str. 22/7—24/8/51.**C/L.**
Str. 2/10—15/11/52.**G.**
Don. 26/1/55. *Not repaired.*

BOILERS:
7019.
7223 19/9/25.
8700 8/4/33.
7758 27/8/38.
7645 1/8/42.
9147 25/11/44.
9634 28/9/46.
9634 reno.21494 24/8/51.
21519 15/11/52.

SHEDS:
Bradford.
Copley Hill 27/3/41.
Bradford 1/4/41.

RENUMBERED:
4574 19/9/25.
9454 28/9/46.
ᴇ**9454** 30/1/48.
69454 20/1/50.

CONDEMNED: 7/2/55.
Cut up at Doncaster.

4575

Doncaster 1290.

To traffic 12/1910.

REPAIRS:
Don. 3/5—28/10/22.**G.**
Don. 2/3—23/5/25.**G.**
Don. 26/11/27—3/3/28.**G.**
Don. 6/9—4/10/30.**G.**
Don. 9/6—14/7/34.**G.**
Don. 6—20/11/37.**G.**
Don. 2—23/11/40.**G.**
Don. 15/1—5/2/44.**G.**
Don. 9/11—6/12/46.**G.**
Don. 14/1—26/2/49.**G.**
Str. 28/8—6/10/51.**G.**
Don. 22/4/55. *Not repaired.*

BOILERS:
7020.
7055 3/3/28.
8196 14/7/34.
9633 6/12/46.
8328 26/2/49.
21501 6/10/51.

SHEDS:
Hornsey.
King's Cross 27/7/34.
Bradford 4/12/42.
Hatfield 5/3/44.
Hornsey 22/12/49.
Colwick 11/4/54.
Hornsey 18/4/54.
Bradford 18/3/55.

RENUMBERED:
4575 23/5/25.
9455 6/10/46.
69455 26/2/49.

CONDEMNED: 16/5/55.
Cut up at Doncaster.

WORKS CODES:- Cw - Cowlairs. Dar- Darlington. Don - Doncaster. Ghd - Gateshead. Gor - Gorton. Hsi - Hull Springhead. Inv - Inverurie. Str - Stratford.
REPAIR CODES:- **C/H** - Casual Heavy. **C/L** - Casual Light. **G** - General. **H**- Heavy. **H/I** - Heavy Intermediate. **L** - Light. **L/I** - Light Intermediate. **N/C** - Non-Classified.

From 1923 to at least July 1930, No.4587 ran without front footsteps and it was also unusual in having the trip cock fitted so far forward. It did have front footsteps put on later. Shireoaks, (Doncaster-Worksop running-in turn) April 1928.

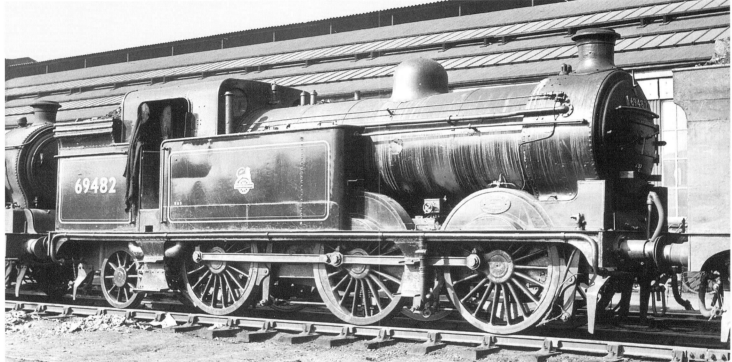

(above) Between September 1950 and January 1953, all trip cocks were moved to the forward position, because London Transport required them to be not more than 5 feet behind leading wheel centre. Stratford shed.

(left) An instruction dated 1st October 1953 ordered trip cock gear to be removed when Class N1 engines left the London area. No.69450 left Hornsey for Copley Hill on 24th June 1951 and by this 12th April 1953 photograph the tripping mechanism had been removed.

Condensing engines had a crosshead driven feed pump between the frames to deliver through clack valves just ahead of the tanks.

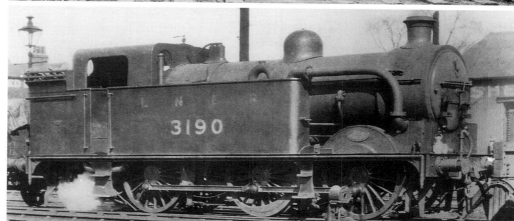

On at least four engines Nos.1561, 3190, 4555 and 4589, the clack valves were fitted on the front ring of the boiler.

Ex-works 7th February 1920, No.1589 was fitted with a Westinghouse feed pump on the right hand side in place of crosshead pump but was the only one so altered.

This Westinghouse pump was retained to January 1948, as were the Ramsbottom safety valves.

4576

Doncaster 1291.

To traffic 12/1910.

REPAIRS:
Don. 9/11/21—1/4/22.**G.**
Don. 6/3—30/5/25.**G.**
Don. 27/8—18/11/27.**G.**
Don. 15/3—12/4/30.**G.**
Don. 28/10—25/11/33.**G.**
Str. 12/12/36—23/1/37.**G.**
Don. 1—22/6/40.**G.**
Don. 16/9—14/10/44.**G.**
Don. 5/3—26/4/48.**G.**
Str. 5/6—4/8/51.**G.**
Don. 2/11/54. *Not repaired.*

BOILERS:
7052.
7756 30/5/25.
8187 25/11/33.
9494 14/10/44.
21489 4/8/51.

SHEDS:
Hornsey.
Ardsley 19/4/53.

RENUMBERED:
4576 30/5/25.
9456 21/9/46.
69456 26/4/48.

CONDEMNED: 15/11/54.
Cut up at Doncaster.

———————————

4577

Doncaster 1292.

To traffic 1/1911.

REPAIRS:
Don. 14/12/21—29/4/22.**G.**
Don. 3/4—6/6/25.**G.**
Don. 11/12/26—12/3/27.**G.**
Don. 31/8—5/10/29.**G.**
Don. 29/8—3/10/31.**G.**
Don. 27/10—10/11/34.**G.**
New pattern axleboxes.
Str. 21/5—25/6/38.**G.**
Don. 12/10—16/11/40.**G.**
Don. 7—28/8/43.**G.**
Don. 30/3—27/4/46.**G.**
Don. 20/11—19/12/47.**G.**
Don. 23/1—18/2/49.**G.**
Str. 31/7—6/9/52.**G.**
Str. 16/3—18/4/53.**C/L.**
Don. 31/1—14/2/55.**C/L.**
Don. 23/4/57. *Not repaired.*

BOILERS:
7053.
D1878 *(new)* 12/3/27.
7997 25/6/38.
7407 16/11/40.
8328 28/8/43.
9633 18/2/49.
21517 6/9/52.

SHEDS:
Hornsey.
Colwick 11/1/39.
Woodford 17/8/39.
Ardsley 7/12/39.
King's Cross 11/2/41.
Hatfield 27/3/41.
Bradford 18/11/45.
Hornsey 20/10/47.
Colwick 7/2/54.
Ardsley 23/10/55.
Bradford 1/4/56.
Copley Hill 10/3/57.

RENUMBERED:
4577 6/6/25.
9457 29/9/46.
69457 18/2/49.

CONDEMNED: 23/4/57.
Cut up at Doncaster.

———————————

4578

Doncaster 1293.

To traffic 1/1911.

REPAIRS:
Don. 5/3—15/5/20.**G.**
Don. 1/3—25/6/23.**G.**
Don. 14/1—11/4/25.**G.**
Don. 3/9—24/11/27.**G.**
Don. 17/5—21/6/30.**G.**
Don. 12/8—9/9/33.**G.**
Don. 8—29/8/36.**G.**
Don. 18/5—15/6/40.**G.**
Don. 20/11/43—1/1/44.**G.**
Don. 29/12/45—2/2/46.**G.**
Don. 21/12/47—12/2/48.**G.**
Str. 25/7—8/9/51.**G.**

BOILERS:
7054.
7754 11/4/25.
8389 21/6/30.
8537 15/6/40.
8529 2/2/46.
21492 8/9/51.

SHEDS:
Hornsey.
Hatfield 9/4/42.
Bradford 18/11/45.
Hornsey 20/10/47.

RENUMBERED:
4578 11/4/25.
9458 6/10/46.
E9458 12/2/48.
69458 8/9/51.

CONDEMNED: 4/11/55.
Cut up at Doncaster.

———————————

4579

Doncaster 1294.

To traffic 2/1911.

REPAIRS:
Don. 10/2—4/7/22.**G.**
Don. 12/2—16/5/25.**G.**
Don. 23/5—30/7/27.**G.**
Don. 5/10—2/11/29.**G.**
Don. 27/9—1/11/30.**G.**
Don. 4—25/2/33.**G.**
Don. 4—25/5/35.**G.**
Fountain lub.
Don. 13/3—3/4/37.**G.**
Don. 28/1—18/2/39.**G.**
Don. 30/8—5/10/41.**G.**
Don. 30/10—20/11/43.**G.**
Don. 23/2—23/3/46.**G.**
Don. 17/3—5/5/48.**G.**
Don. 26/3—3/5/50.**G.**
Str. 25/8—4/10/52.**G.**

BOILERS:
7055.
8001 30/7/27.
7645 25/5/35.
9271 5/10/41.
9273 3/5/50.
21520 4/10/52.

SHEDS:
King's Cross.
Ardsley 17/7/27.
Hatfield 4/3/31.
King's Cross 14/5/34.
Hatfield 31/1/36.
Ardsley 15/10/37.
Bradford 27/10/37.
Hatfield 16/10/39.
Bradford 17/10/43.

RENUMBERED:
4579 16/5/25.
9459 22/9/46.
69459 5/5/48.

CONDEMNED: 28/3/55.
Cut up at Doncaster.

———————————

4580

Doncaster 1295.

To traffic 2/1911.

REPAIRS:
Don. 27/10—4/3/22.**G.**
Don. 27/10—31/1/25.**G.**
Don. 28/2—14/5/27.**G.**
Don. 15/2—22/3/30.**G.**
Don. 30/7—3/9/32.**G.**
Don. 27/7—24/8/35.**G.**
Fountain lub.
Str. 13/3—28/4/39.**G.**
Don. 16/10—27/11/43.**G.**
Don. 19/3—4/5/47.**G.**
Str. 18/2—21/4/51.**G.**
Str. 19—22/5/51.**N/C.**
Str. 21/12/51—11/1/52.**C/L.**

BOILERS:
7056.
6930 14/5/27.
8335 22/3/30.
8416 28/4/39.
8388 4/5/47.
21482 21/4/51.

SHED:
Hornsey.

RENUMBERED:
4580 31/1/25.
9460 13/10/46.
69460 21/4/51.

CONDEMNED: 22/8/55.
Cut up at Doncaster.

———————————

4581

Doncaster 1326.

To traffic 12/1911.

REPAIRS:
Don. 23/8—30/12/22.**G.**
Don. 28/7—10/10/25.**G.**
Don. 17/3—4/7/28.**G.**
Don. 10/8—7/9/29.**G.**
Don. 26/12/31—23/1/32.**G.**
Don. 29/9—20/10/34.**G.**
Don. 25/9—9/10/37.**G.**
Don. 1—22/2/41.**G.**
Don. 8—29/1/44.**G.**
Don. 28/9—30/10/47.**G.**
Str. 3/10—25/11/50.**G.**
Str. 29/10—14/11/51.**C/H.**
Str. 20/6—11/8/53.**C/L.**
Str. 27/5/54. *Not repaired.*

BOILERS:
7102.

Although reported in June 1925 as very satisfactory and reliable, no other than 1589 got a steam driven feed pump. The crosshead pumps were removed in 1926-29 and replaced by under-footplate injectors.

Coupled axles were originally lubricated by oil boxes mounted on the front end of the side tanks.

Between 1934 and 1937 many got new axleboxes and these were oil fed from a fountain lubricator mounted in the cab.

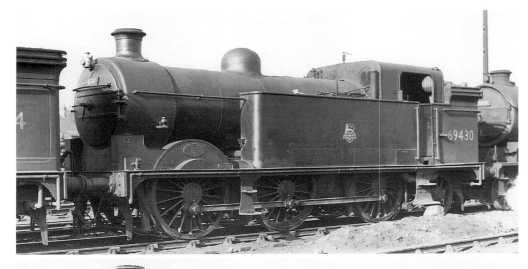

On the others, the oil boxes on the front end of the tanks were retained to withdrawal. The cylinders and valves were fed from displacement lubricators mounted on the sides of the smokebox. Cambridge, 26th October 1952.

From new until July 1933 No.3190 had its displacement lubricators on the front of the smokebox. Ex-works 29th July 1933 it had been brought into line with the others as shown in the illustration on page 28, second from top.

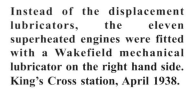

Instead of the displacement lubricators, the eleven superheated engines were fitted with a Wakefield mechanical lubricator on the right hand side. King's Cross station, April 1938.

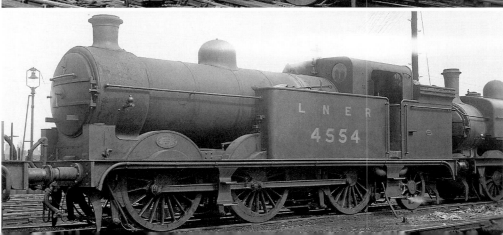

Until 1933 normal sanding was steam applied in front of leading, and by gravity behind trailing coupled wheels.

4581 cont./
6933 30/12/22.
D1888 *(exD2 4384)* 20/10/34.
7995 9/10/37.
21475 25/11/50.
21503 14/11/51.

SHEDS:
King's Cross.
Ardsley 15/2/43.

RENUMBERED:
4581 10/10/25.
9461 29/9/46.
69461 25/11/50.

CONDEMNED: 7/6/54.
Cut up at Stratford.

_____

4582

Doncaster 1327.

To traffic 12/1911.

REPAIRS:
Don. 20/5—15/10/21.**G.**
Don. 9/4—5/7/24.**G.**
Don. 16/3—14/7/26.**G.**
Don. 11/7—27/9/28.**G.**
Don. 21/11—12/12/31.**G.**
Don. 16/6—14/7/34.**G.**
Str. 3/10—7/11/36.**G.**
Str. 30/11—23/12/38.**G.**
Don. 1/2—1/3/41.**G.**
Don. 18/11—9/12/44.**G.**
Don. 11/10—25/11/48.**G.**
Str. 21/4—30/5/52.**G.**
Str. 27/6—3/7/52.**N/C.**
Don. 13/2—17/3/56.**G.**
Don. 31/3/59. *Not repaired.*

BOILERS:
7103.
7150 14/7/26.
7399 7/11/36.
8532 23/12/38.
8468 1/3/41.
8729 25/11/48.
21491 30/5/52.
21472 17/3/56.

SHEDS:
King's Cross.
Ardsley 13/6/26.
Hornsey 21/7/26.
Hatfield 25/11/32.
Hornsey 28/2/40.
King's Cross 12/9/42.
Hornsey 11/3/48.
Copley Hill 28/6/53.
Hatfield 15/8/54.
King's Cross 29/8/54.
Hatfield 19/9/54.

Hornsey 15/5/55.
Copley Hill 19/5/57.

RENUMBERED:
4582 5/7/24.
9462 6/10/46.
69462 25/11/48.

CONDEMNED: 3/4/59.
Cut up at Doncaster.

_____

4583

Doncaster 1328.

To traffic 12/1911.

REPAIRS:
Don. 13/6—14/11/22.**G.**
Don. 16/1—25/4/25.**G.**
Don. 12/8—21/10/27.**G.**
Don. 12/10—9/11/29.**G.**
Don. 5/3—2/4/32.**G.**
Don. 3—24/11/34.**G.**
New pattern axleboxes fitted.
Str. 19/3—7/5/38.**G.**
Don. 5—26/6/43.**G.**
Don. 18/11/46—11/1/47.**G.**
Str. 12/7—9/9/50.**G.**
Str. 18/8—12/9/52.**G.**
Don. 24/10/55. *Not repaired.*

BOILERS:
7104.
7997 21/10/27.
8412 7/5/38.
8536 26/6/43.
21471 9/9/50.
21514 12/9/52.

SHEDS:
King's Cross.
Hornsey 8/10/38.
Ardsley 24/6/51.

RENUMBERED:
4583 25/4/25.
9463 20/10/46.
69463 9/9/50.

CONDEMNED: 28/10/55.
Cut up at Doncaster.

_____

4584

Doncaster 1329.

To traffic 1/1912.

REPAIRS:
Don. 12/8—23/10/20.**G.**
Don. 16/11/23—8/3/24.**G.**
Don. 4/10/26—8/1/27.**G.**

Don. 23/2—6/4/29.**G.**
Don. 18/7—22/8/31.**G.**
Don. 20/1—17/2/34.**G.**
Str. 22/8—10/10/36.**G.**
Str. 30/8—30/9/38.**G.**
Don. 30/8—27/9/41.**G.**
Don. 7—28/10/44.**G.**
Don. 20/4—5/6/47.**G.**
Don. 21/7—12/8/48.**L.**
Don. 14/8—30/9/49.**G.**
Str. 2/11—15/12/51.**G.**
Str. 15/11—4/12/52.**C/L.**
Str. 9/12/53—13/2/54.**G.**

BOILERS:
7105.
7674 *(Sup.)* 8/3/24.
8716 17/2/34.
9058 30/9/38.
8997 5/6/47.
21504 15/12/51.
21240 13/2/54.

SHEDS:
Hornsey.
Hatfield 1/5/43.
Bradford 19/12/43.

RENUMBERED:
4584 8/3/24.
9464 6/10/46.
69464 12/8/48.

CONDEMNED: 8/8/55.
Cut up at Doncaster.

_____

4585

Doncaster 1330.

To traffic 1/1912.

REPAIRS:
Don. 8/12/21—6/5/22.**G.**
Don. 18/8—8/11/24.**G.**
Don. 15/2—14/4/27.**G.**
Don. 30/11—28/12/29.**G.**
Don. 11/3—8/4/33.**G.**
Rail washing gear fitted.
Don. 8—29/2/36.**G.**
Don. 2/12/39—6/1/40.**G.**
Don. 31/1—14/2/42.**L.**
Str. 11/11/42—3/4/43.*Spec.*
Don. 3—31/3/45.**G.**
Don. 8/6—28/7/48.**G.**
Str. 8/12/51—19/1/52.**G.**
Str. 10/11—1/12/52.**C/L.**

BOILERS:
7106.
7994 14/4/27.
8878 29/2/36.
8879 28/7/48.
21507 19/1/52.

SHED:
Hornsey.

RENUMBERED:
4585 8/11/24.
9465 28/9/46.
69465 28/7/48.

CONDEMNED: 10/12/55.
Cut up at Doncaster.

_____

4586

Doncaster 1331.

To traffic 2/1912.

REPAIRS:
Don. 29/3—29/7/22.**G.**
Don. 1/7—1/11/24.**G.**
Don. 7/2—30/4/27.**G.**
Don. 5/10—2/11/29.**G.**
Don. 13/8—24/9/32.**G.**
Don. 11/1—1/2/36.**G.**
Don. 4/11—9/12/39.**G.**
Don. 13/5—10/6/44.**G.**
Don. 11/10—14/11/47.**G.**
Str. 4/4—23/5/51.**G.**
Don. 21/6/55. *Not repaired.*

BOILERS:
7107.
D1875 *(new)* 30/4/27.
8531 10/6/44.
21486 23/5/51.

SHEDS:
Hornsey.
King's Cross 14/9/42.
Hornsey 16/12/48.

RENUMBERED:
4586 1/11/24.
9466 11/10/46.
69466 23/5/51.

CONDEMNED: 4/7/55.
Cut up at Doncaster.

_____

4587

Doncaster 1332.

To traffic 2/1912.

Sold to War Office 10/12/14.
Repurchased 3/3/23.

REPAIRS:
Don. 28/2—13/5/23.**G.**
Lined black, lettered L&NER.
Don. 17/9—14/11/25.**G.**
Don. 18/1—28/3/28.**G.**

Ex-works 25th March 1933, No.4562, and 4565 on 8th April 1933, had been changed to gravity sanding at the front, because rail-washing gear had been put on. Dates when this was removed have not been found. Doncaster station.

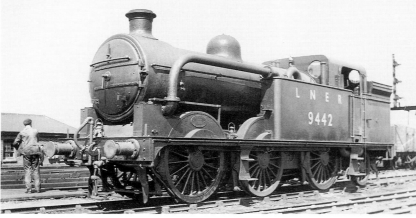

Although both had the rail washing gear removed (probably in 1939), they kept gravity sanding at the front. No.4562 became 9442 on 13th September 1946.

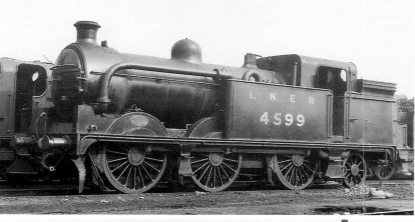

On superheated engines which had condensing gear - only 4572 and 4592 did not - the top part of the front sandboxes had to be cut back by 4in. because the pipe exit point had to be moved forward. When condensing gear was removed, the sandbox was unaltered (see page 39, middle) but, the illustration on page 14, top, shows a normal sandbox was restored to 69436.

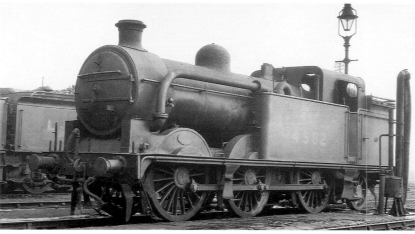

Nos.4561 to 4570 (only) had 4in. smaller rear cab windows due to use of some existing 14in. diameter stock, and they only had four protection bars.

Otherwise five vertical bars was standard protection for the rear windows of the cab. High Barnet, May 1923.

From March 1935 the bars had to be increased to seven due to more breakages at mechanical coaling plants. Hither Green.

Until April 1924 there was no handrail around the bunker to assist movement there. King's Cross shed.

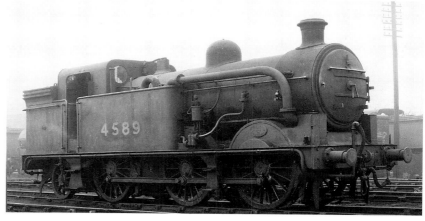

From then onwards, all had a handrail fitted along each side and around the back of the bunker.

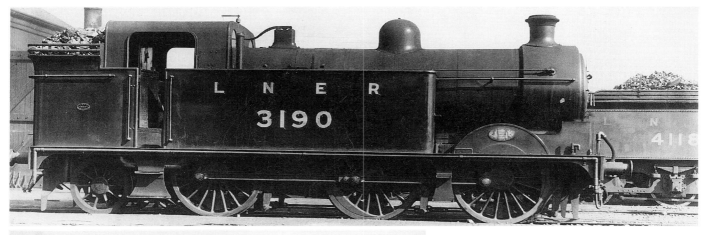

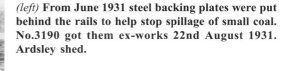

(above) **Until June 1931 only two open coal rails were provided on the bunker top. Ardsley shed.**

(left) **From June 1931 steel backing plates were put behind the rails to help stop spillage of small coal. No.3190 got them ex-works 22nd August 1931. Ardsley shed.**

The plate across the back impeded the view when in reverse and later was cut back in width (*see* previous page, second from top) or removed completely as here. Bradford Exchange.

Until into early LNER days the handrail across the smokebox door remained in its original position below the upper hinge strap. King's Cross station.

By October 1923 the rail had begun to be moved above the upper strap and all were so altered.

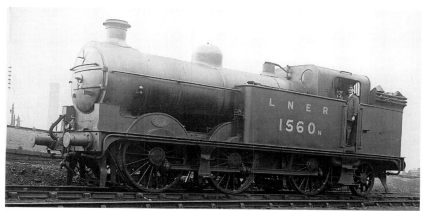

Boilers built after 1926 were fitted with Ross 'pop' safety valves instead of the Ramsbottom type. No.4577, ex-works 12th March 1927, was the first N1 with 'pop' valves.

Ex-works 15th October 1921, No.1582 had been fitted with a Westinghouse brake pump for testing East Coast Joint Stock carriages at King's Cross. No.4582 still had the pump in December 1944 but it had gone by November 1948. King's Cross station, 26th May 1923.

Also in October 1921 No.1581 was fitted with a Westinghouse brake pump for ECJS testing. This was done at King's Cross shed, the pump having previously been on 0-4-4T No.767. No.4581 is believed to have kept the pump to September 1947. King's Cross shed, June 1925.

Otherwise, the whole class just had vacuum brake for engine and for train working. Until 1931 the ejector exhaust pipe was through the boiler but then became external along the right hand side. Bradford (Bowling) shed.

4587 cont./
Don. 5/7—9/8/30.**G.**
Don. 3—24/12/32.**G.**
Don. 4—25/7/36.**G.**
Don. 2/12/39—6/1/40.**G.**
Don. 10—31/10/42.**G.**
Don. 27/10—1/12/45.**G.**
Don. 12/5—14/6/49.**G.**
Str. 3/11—6/12/52.**G.**
Don. 12—24/9/55.**C/L.**

BOILERS:
7108.
7019 14/11/25.
7998 24/12/32.
8881 25/7/36.
9007 14/6/49.
21508 6/12/52.

SHEDS:
King's Cross 13/5/23.
Hatfield 1/3/29.
King's Cross 7/4/31.
Hornsey 11/3/48.
Colwick 11/4/54.
Bradford 10/4/55.

RENUMBERED:
4587 14/11/25.
9467 11/10/46.
69467 14/6/49.

CONDEMNED: 2/7/56.
Cut up a Doncaster.

4588

Doncaster 1333.

To traffic 2/1912.

REPAIRS:
Don. 8/5—14/10/22.**G.**
Don. 26/1—11/4/25.**G.**
Don. 4/4—11/6/27.**G.**
Don. 4/5—8/6/29.**G.**
Don. 27/6—25/7/31.**G.**
Don. 3—17/11/34.**G.**
New pattern axleboxes fitted.
Str. 25/6—23/7/38.**G.**
Don. 6—19/12/39.**G.**
Don. 19/4—17/5/41.**G.**
Str. 21/8—12/9/42.**L.**
Don. 2—23/9/44.**G.**
Don. 1/4—6/5/48.**G.**
Str. 5/6—18/8/51.**G.**
Str. 27/10—25/11/52.**N/C.**
Don. 27/1/54. *Not repaired.*

BOILERS:
7109.
7149 11/6/27.
8728 17/11/34.
D1878 *(ex4577)* 23/7/38.

7997 17/5/41.
21488 18/8/51.

SHEDS:
Hornsey.
Ardsley 11/6/29.
King's Cross 24/7/31.
Hornsey 19/8/31.
Colwick 11/1/39.
Woodford 31/7/39.
Ardsley 6/12/39.
Bradford 23/12/39.
King's Cross 12/4/41.
Hatfield 11/3/48.
Hornsey 22/12/49.
King's Cross 31/5/53.
Hornsey 5/7/53.
Copley Hill 12/7/53.

RENUMBERED:
4588 11/4/25.
9468 12/10/46.
69468 6/5/48.

CONDEMNED: 8/3/54.
Cut up at Doncaster.

4589

Doncaster 1334.

To traffic 2/1912.

REPAIRS:
Don. ?/?—7/2/20.**G.**
Westinghouse feed pump fitted.
Don. 27/11/22—12/3/23.**G.**
Green livery, lettered L&NER.
Don. 31/3—30/5/25.**G.**
Don. 12/8—8/11/27.**G.**
Don. 14/12/29—18/1/30.**G.**
Don. 26/8—30/9/33.**G.**
Don. 27/2—13/3/37.**G.**
Don. 12/10—9/11/40.**G.**
Don. 25/3—22/2/44.**G.**
Don. 29/1—27/2/48.**G.**
Str. 14/8—15/9/51.**C/L.**
Str. 20/1—1/3/52.**G.**
Str. 17—21/3/52.**N/C.**
Don. 2/4/57. *Not repaired.*

BOILERS:
7110.
1322 7/2/20.
7757 30/5/25.
7755 30/9/33.
9278 27/2/48.
21509 1/3/52.

SHEDS:
King's Cross.
Hornsey 17/10/30.
Hatfield 29/1/42.
King's Cross 26/12/43.

Hornsey 16/12/48.
Colwick 7/2/54.
Staveley 28/3/54.
Colwick 31/10/54.
Ardsley 23/10/55.
Copley Hill 4/11/56.

RENUMBERED:
4589 30/5/25.
9469 28/9/46.
ᴇ9469 27/2/48.
69469 15/9/51.

CONDEMNED: 15/4/57.
Cut up at Doncaster.

4590

Doncaster 1335.

To traffic 3/1912.

Sold to War Office 31/3/15.
Repurchased 3/3/23.

REPAIRS:
Don. 28/2—4/6/23.**G.**
Lined black, lettered L&NER..
Don. 6/10—5/12/25.**G.**
Don. 5/3—16/6/28.**G.**
Don. 19/4—24/5/30.**G.**
Don. 3/9—8/10/32.**G.**
Don. 6—27/4/35.**G.**
Fountain lub.
Don. 25/2—1/4/39.**G.**
Don. 16/10—6/11/43.**G.**
Don. 19/5—16/6/45.**G.**
Don. 24/8—1/10/48.**G.**
Str. 13/1—16/2/52.**G.**
Don. 23/7/56. *Not repaired.*

BOILERS:
7111.
7410 24/5/30.
8192 1/4/39.
8709 16/6/45.
21499 16/2/52.

SHEDS:
King's Cross 4/6/23.
Hatfield 5/3/29.
King's Cross 30/6/29.
Hatfield 20/10/29.
King's Cross 9/3/31.
Hitchin 19/10/31.
Hatfield 14/1/33.
King's Cross 9/9/33.
Hornsey 11/5/35.
King's Cross 31/5/53.
Hornsey 5/7/53.

RENUMBERED:
4590 5/12/25.
9470 20/10/46.

69470 1/10/48.

CONDEMNED: 6/8/56.
Cut up at Doncaster.

4591

Doncaster 1336.

To traffic 3/1912.

REPAIRS:
Don. 13/2—29/6/23.**G.**
Don. 29/10/25—19/1/26.**G.**
Don. 21/2—13/7/28.**G.**
Don. 23/8—4/10/30.**G.**
Don. 8—29/7/33.**G.**
Str. 19/9—24/10/36.**G.**
Don. 13/7—3/8/40.**G.**
Don. 5—26/8/44.**G.**
Don. 4/12/47—5/1/48.**G.**
Str. 25/7—30/9/50.**G.**
Str. 13/10—21/11/53.**G.**
Don. 12/1—5/2/54.**C/L.**
Don. 28/12/55. *Not repaired.*

BOILERS:
7112.
7399 13/7/28.
8883 24/10/36.
21472 30/9/50.
21528 21/11/53.

SHEDS:
Hornsey.
Copley Hill 5/4/46.
Bradford 15/8/54.

RENUMBERED:
4591 ?/3/25.
9471 27/10/46.
69471 30/9/50.

CONDEMNED: 16/1/56.
Cut up at Doncaster.

4592

Doncaster 1338.

To traffic 4/1912.

REPAIRS:
Don. 28/3—12/8/22.**G.**
Don. 8/12/24—7/3/25.**G.**
Don. 30/12/27—9/5/28.**G.**
Don. 4/10—8/11/30.**G.**
Don. 19/8—23/9/33.**G.**
Don. 19/10—16/11/35.**G.**
Don. 6—27/11/37.**G.**
Don. 2—23/3/40.**G.**
Don. 1—22/5/43.**G.**
Don. 13/10—17/11/45.**G.**

(above) **From July 1925, when trip cock's began to be fitted, it was just ahead of the radial wheel on both sides of the engine except for the isolated case of No.4587 (*see* page 20, top).**

(right) **During the 1914-18 war some were painted grey with single white lining but it is believed that by Grouping all were in fully lined green passenger livery. King's Cross shed, July 1920.**

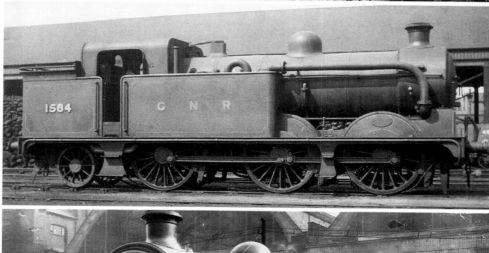

No.1581, ex-Doncaster on 30th December 1922, was the last one to get the GNR initials which it kept until it went to works on 28th July 1925. King's Cross station.

The Great Northern style was continued for Nos.1601 (15th February 1923) and 1604 (16th February 1923) the only change being from GNR to L&NER initials, and the bunker back numbering was still to be seen. Note that GNR lining panels had scalloped corners. King's Cross shed.

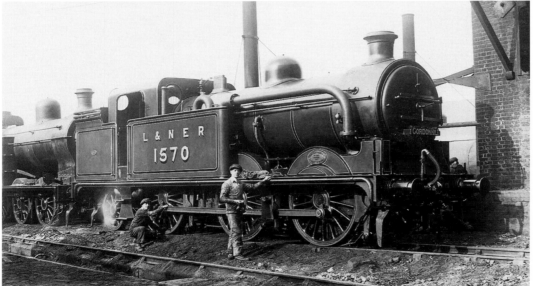

Three more were painted green with black and white lining but with rounded corners to the panels. The number was now on the tank sides and increased to 12in. figures under 7$\frac{1}{2}$in. L&NER, all in gold, shaded red, transfers. Those to get this style, all in 1923, were Nos.1570 (26th February), 1605 (5th March) and 1589 (12th March). King's Cross shed, 3rd March 1923.

With only 5ft 8in. wheels, N1 class was included in the classes to be black with single red lining, and the first paintings still had the ampersand in the company's initials. Three got this style in April 1923, Nos.1571 (5th), 1565 (7th) and 1600 (14th), followed by No.1587 on the 13th May and 1590 on 4th June. Although mainly passenger engines, they worked goods trains to the Southern Railway yards at Feltham and Hither Green. Some thus carried GNR load Class F collar on the vacuum standpipe.

4592 cont./
Don. 29/12/45—5/1/46.**L.**
Don. 9/8—15/9/49.**G.**
Str. 13/6—14/8/52.**G.**
Str. 5—19/9/52.**N/C.**
Don. 10/3—6/4/55.**G.**
Don. 19/8/58. *Not repaired.*

BOILERS:
7113.
D1749 *(new & sup.)* 9/5/28.
8543 27/11/37.
8404 15/9/49.
21516 14/8/52.
21287 6/4/55.

SHEDS:
Copley Hill.
Ardsley 17/8/41.
Copley Hill 2/11/41.
Ardsley 4/3/51.

RENUMBERED:
4592 7/3/25.
9472 20/10/46.
69472 15/9/49.

CONDEMNED: 21/8/58.
Cut up at Doncaster.

_____

4593

Doncaster 1337.

To traffic 3/1912.

REPAIRS:
Don. 25/10/20—5/3/21.**G.**
Don. 19/3—21/7/23.**G.**
Don. 6/10/25—15/1/26.**G.**
Don. 13/4—11/6/27.**G.**
Don. 29/6—10/8/29.**G.**
Don. 30/7—27/8/32.**G.**
Don. 2—23/3/35.**G.**
Fountain lub.
Don. 20/3—3/4/37.**G.**
Don. 15/4—13/5/39.**G.**
Don. 18/10—15/11/41.**G.**
Don. 5—19/2/44.**G.**
Don. 4/5—1/6/46.**G.**
Don. 17/3—8/4/49.**G.**
Don. 29/6—19/7/51.**C/L.**
Str. 21/11—29/12/51.**C/L.**
Don. 17/8/52. *Not repaired.*

BOILERS:
7114.
7995 11/6/27.
9001 3/4/37.
9272 15/11/41.
9632 1/6/46.
9632 reno.21508 29/12/51.

SHEDS:
Bradford.
Ardsley 26/3/41.
Bradford 8/4/41.
Ardsley 6/9/44.
Copley Hill 5/12/48.

RENUMBERED:
4593 10/2/25.
9473 26/10/46.
69473 8/4/49.

CONDEMNED: 1/9/52.
Cut up at Doncaster.

_____

4594

Doncaster 1339.

To traffic 4/1912.

REPAIRS:
Don. 29/8—19/11/21.**G.**
Don. 4/2—31/5/24.**G.**
Don. 20/4—12/8/26.**G.**
Don. 20/8—24/10/28.**G.**
Don. 3—31/1/31.**G.**
Don. 24/12/32—28/1/33.**G.**
Don. 6/1—3/2/34.**G.**
Don. 13/7—3/8/35.**G.**
Fountain lub.
Don. 3—24/7/37.**G.**
Don. 25/11—23/12/39.**G.**
Don. 10/10—7/11/42.**G.**
Don. 19/5—23/6/45.**G.**
Don. 2/1—8/2/47.**L.**
Don. 31/8—27/10/47.**G.**
Don. 26/8—19/10/49.**G.**
Str. 16/10—30/11/51.**G.**
Don. 15/2—16/3/54.**G.**
Don. 28/3—10/5/56.**G.**

BOILERS:
7115.
6853 12/8/26.
8736 3/8/35.
8728 27/10/47.
21496 30/11/51.
21481 16/3/54.
21485 10/5/56.

SHEDS:
Bradford.
Ardsley 6/10/57.

RENUMBERED:
4594 31/5/24.
9474 28/7/46.
69474 19/10/49.

CONDEMNED: 13/3/59.
Into Don. for cut up 16/3/59.

_____

4595

Doncaster 1340.

To traffic 4/1912.

REPAIRS:
Don. 15/5—21/10/22.**G.**
Don. 23/1—25/4/25.**G.**
Don. 13/4—25/6/27.**G.**
Don. 11/5—15/6/29.**G.**
Don. 18/7—15/8/31.**G.**
Don. 28/4—26/5/34.**G.**
Str. 20/11—11/12/37.**G.**
Don. 6/12/41—10/1/42.**G.**
Don. 22/4—18/5/44.**G.**
Don. 5/10—13/11/47.**G.**
Str. 18/3—3/5/51.**G.**
Str. 29/12/52—21/2/53.**H/I.**

BOILERS:
7116.
7001 25/6/27.
8705 26/5/34.
9003 11/12/37.
8533 13/11/47.
21484 3/5/51.

SHEDS:
Bradford.
Hornsey 14/8/31.
Bradford 22/2/53.
Hatfield 15/8/54.
King's Cross 22/8/54.
Hatfield 19/9/54.
Copley Hill 20/2/55.
Bradford 6/3/55.

RENUMBERED:
4595 25/4/25.
9475 17/3/46.
69475 3/5/51.

CONDEMNED: 11/4/55.

_____

4596

Doncaster 1341.

To traffic 5/1912.

REPAIRS:
Don. 6/5—17/7/20.**G.**
Don. 18/4—12/8/23.**G.**
Don. 7/8—17/10/25.**G.**
Don. 13/12/27—4/3/28.**G.**
Don. 1/2—1/3/30.**G.**
Don. 30/4—28/5/32.**G.**
Don. 11/5—1/6/35.**G.**
Str. 17/10—18/11/38.**G.**
Str. 21/8—7/11/42.**G.**
Don. 25/11—9/12/44.**G.**
Don. 5/4—13/5/48.**G.**

Str. 22/6—7/8/51.**C/L.**
Str. 12/2—22/3/52.**G.**
Str. 21/10—26/11/53.**C/L.**

BOILERS:
7142.
6925 4/3/28.
8532 28/5/32.
8332 18/11/38.
8417 13/5/48.
21512 22/3/52.

SHEDS:
King's Cross.
Hornsey 16/1/50.
Colwick 11/4/54.

RENUMBERED:
4596 18/3/25.
9476 18/10/46.
69476 13/5/48.

CONDEMNED: 14/3/55.

_____

4597

Doncaster 1342.

To traffic 5/1912.

REPAIRS:
Don. 29/7—2/10/20.**G.**
Don. 23/8—22/12/23.**G.**
Don. 6/10—12/12/25.**G.**
Don. 4/6—7/12/28.**G.**
Don. 22/8—26/9/31.**G.**
Don. 9/12/33—13/1/34.**G.**
Str. 31/10—28/11/36.**G.**
Don. 8—22/6/40.**G.**
Don. 6—27/5/44.**G.**
Don. 2/11—12/12/47.**G.**
Str. 14/8—29/9/51.**G.**
Don. 2/5—9/6/56.**G.**
Don. 12—27/12/56.**C/L.**
Don. 31/3/59. *Not repaired.*

BOILERS:
7143.
7112 7/12/28.
8417 28/11/36.
9355 12/12/47.
21497 29/9/51.
21481 9/6/56.

SHEDS:
King's Cross.
Hornsey 30/6/29.
Copley Hill 14/9/52.
Hatfield 15/8/54.
King's Cross 29/8/54.
Hatfield 19/9/54.
Hornsey 30/1/55.
Copley Hill 16/6/57.

During June 1923, it was decided to cease using the ampersand, but the original number was continued. Three got this style, Nos.1552 (14th July), 1569 (9th August) and 1558 (22nd August), all in 1923. No.1578, ex-works 25th June 1923 was probably also in this style, as would be 1591 (29th June), 1599 (17th July), 1593 (21st July), and 1596 (12th August).

Because Group records were being confused by more than one engine having the same number (North Eastern and Great Eastern each also had a No.1554), from late August 1923 a sectional suffix was introduced and was applied until February 1924, N1 class getting an N. Those to do so were Nos.1551, 1554, 1560, 1561, 1564, 1566, 1568, 1597, 1598 and 1602 between 22nd September 1923 and 16th February 1924. Bradford Exchange.

LNER renumbering began with No.4603 ex-works 23rd February 1924 and the red lining continued to be applied until war conditions caused its demise from November 1941. Doncaster, September 1932.

From July 1942 the 7½in. LNER gave way to NE but for this 12in. letters were used. Copley Hill shed, April 1946.

4597 cont./
RENUMBERED:
 1597N 22/12/23.
 4597 12/12/25.
 9477 25/10/46.
 69477 29/9/51.

CONDEMNED: 2/4/59.
Cut up at Doncaster.

_____

4598

Doncaster 1343.

To traffic 5/1912.

REPAIRS:
Don. ?/?—23/2/18.**G.**
Don. 29/7—16/10/20.**G.**
Don. 23/8—27/11/23.**G.**
Don. 16/12/25—6/3/26.**G.**
Don. 29/2—8/6/28.**G.**
Don. 5/4—10/5/30.**G.**
Don. 29/10—19/11/32.**G.**
Don. 9—30/3/35.**G.**
Fountain lub.
Str. 26/12/36—30/1/37.**G.**
Don. 6—27/1/40.**G.**
Don. 15/1—5/2/44.**G.**
Don. 6—20/5/44.**L.**
Don. 10—17/6/44.**L.**
Don. 18/8—22/9/45.**G.**
Don. 2/7—26/8/47.**G.**
Don. 16/3—20/4/49.**G.**
Str. 1/8—22/9/51.**G.**
Str. 21/8—3/10/53.**G.**
Str. 4/1—5/3/54.**C/L.**
Don. 15/3—5/4/55.**C/L.**

BOILERS:
 7144.
 7324 *(sup.)* 23/2/18.
 8567 19/11/32.
 8986 30/1/37.
 9328 26/8/47.
 8401 20/4/49.
 21495 22/9/51.
 21526 3/10/53.

SHEDS:
Hornsey.
Bradford 23/9/43.

RENUMBERED:
 1598N 27/11/23.
 4598 6/3/26.
 9478 20/10/46.
 69478 20/4/49.

CONDEMNED: 12/12/56.
Cut up at Doncaster.

_____

4599

Doncaster 1344.

To traffic 5/1912.

REPAIRS:
Don. 1/7—28/8/20.**G.**
Don. 21/2—17/7/23.**G.**
Don. 7/8—24/10/25.**G.**
Don. 13/12/27—2/6/28.**G.**
Don. 15/3—12/4/30.**G.**
Don. 11/6—2/7/32.**G.**
Don. 9—23/2/35.**G.**
Fountain lub.
Don. 1—29/5/37.**G.**
Don. 6—27/4/40.**G.**
Don. 13/11—11/12/43.**G.**
Don. 2/2—9/3/46.**G.**
Don. 18/6—23/7/48.**G.**
Str. 6/9—26/10/50.**G.**

BOILERS:
 7145.
D1752 *(new & sup.)* 2/6/28.
D1744 *(exJ6 3610)* 9/3/46.
 21473 26/10/50.

SHEDS:
King's Cross.
Hornsey 16/9/32.
King's Cross 7/11/32.
Bradford 6/12/43.

RENUMBERED:
 4599 ?/3/25.
 9479 27/10/46.
 69479 23/7/48.

CONDEMNED: 27/10/52.

_____

4600

Doncaster 1345.

To traffic 5/1912.

REPAIRS:
Don. 8/11/22—14/4/23.**G.**
Don. 12/6—29/8/25.**G.**
Don. 19/11/27—11/2/28.**G.**
Don. 8/2—8/3/30.**G.**
Don. 11/6—2/7/32.**G.**
Don. 6—27/4/35.**G.**
Str. 2—31/8/38.**G.**
Don. 8/3—5/4/41.**G.**
Don. 27/5—17/6/44.**G.**
Don. 6/4—27/6/47.**G.**
Str. 21/5/51. *Not repaired.*

BOILERS:
7146.
7144 11/2/28.
8332 8/3/30.
8728 31/8/38.
9804 27/6/47.

SHEDS:
King's Cross.
Hatfield 14/3/29.
King's Cross 6/11/30.
Hornsey 16/1/50.

RENUMBERED:
 4600 29/8/25.
 9480 21/9/46.

CONDEMNED: 25/6/51.
Cut up at Stratford.

_____

4601

Doncaster 1346.

To traffic 5/1912.

REPAIRS:
Don. 18/10/22—15/2/23.**G.**
*In GNR green but lettered
L&NER.*
Don. 12/6—26/9/25.**G.**
Don. 3/12/27—15/3/28.**G.**
Don. 12/10—2/11/29.**G.**
Don. 20/2—19/3/32.**G.**
Don. 6/4—4/5/35.**G.**
*Fountain lub.
Boiler with 'Sinuflo' tubes.*
Don. 27/8—17/9/38.**G.**
Don. 3—17/10/42.**G.**
Don. 13—27/10/45.**G.**
Don. 18/3—28/4/47.**G.**
Don. 19/4—26/5/48.**G.**
Str. 12/7—17/8/51.**C/L.**
Str. 24/11/52—8/1/53.**G.**
Str. 8—15/3/53.**N/C.**

BOILERS:
 7147.
 7116 15/3/28.
 7996 4/5/35.
 8729 17/10/42.
 8466 26/5/48.
 8466 reno.21493 17/8/51.
 21522 8/1/53.

SHEDS:
King's Cross.
Hatfield 8/3/29.
Hornsey 8/4/31.
King's Cross 11/5/35.
Hornsey 16/1/50.
Colwick 3/1/54.
Ardsley 23/10/55.

RENUMBERED:
 4601 26/9/25.
 9481 27/7/46.
 69481 26/5/48.

CONDEMNED: 28/5/56.

_____

4602

Doncaster 1347.

To traffic 6/1912.

REPAIRS:
Don. 18/8—16/10/20.**G.**
Don. 5/9/23—9/3/24.**G.**
Don. 26/7—23/10/26.**G.**
Don. 6/7—10/8/29.**G.**
Don. 20/8—1/10/32.**G.**
Kx. 6/12/32. *Trip cock gear
fitted.*
Don. 2—23/3/35.**G.**
Fountain lub fitted.
Don. 25/9—9/10/37.**G.**
Don. 20/4—18/5/40.**G.**
Don. 12/2—4/3/44.**G.**
Don. 10/11—8/12/45.**G.**
Don. 15/2—25/3/47.**G.**
Don. 31/1—20/2/48.**G.**
Don. 21/3—2/5/50.**G.**
Str. 12/8—20/9/52.**G.**
Don. 1/854. *Not repaired.*

BOILERS:
 7148.
 7677 *(sup.)* 9/3/24.
D1765 *(J6 ex3575)* 1/10/32.
 9262 8/12/45.
 9054 2/5/50.
 21518 20/9/52.

SHEDS:
King's Cross.
Bradford 24/10/26.
King's Cross 27/9/32.
Hatfield 7/11/32.
King's Cross 9/9/33.
Bradford 22/9/43.

RENUMBERED:
 1602N *by* 16/2/24.
 4602 21/2/25.
 9482 7/7/46.
 E**9482** 20/2/48.
 69482 2/5/50.

CONDEMNED: 30/8/54.
Cut up at Doncaster.

_____

4603

Doncaster 1348.

To traffic 6/1912.

REPAIRS:
Don. 17/6—21/8/20.**G.**
Don. 30/10/23—23/2/24.**G.**

In January 1946 LNER was restored, again by 7½in. transfers, and the renumbering from 9430 to 9485 began. No.4569 had LNER restored when ex-works 16th March 1946 but on Sunday 22nd September 1946 Bradford shed, using 6in. stencils, changed it to 9449. Keighley, October 1946.

Transfers and shading continued when stocks were still available and No.9439 ex-works on 18th January 1947 was so treated. Hornsey shed.

The same sizes and position were used when change was made to yellow painted and unshaded characters, No.9484 having them ex-works 18th June 1947.

In January 1948 the new owners had their name put on the tanks, so the number (after 25 years) reverted to the bunker. It also got a prefix letter to indicate to which BR Region it belonged. The first four E9448 (23rd), E9451 (23rd), E9454 (30th), all January 1948, and E9452 (4th February) had the letter in front of the number. Bradford Exchange, April 1949.

There was then a small change of style and the other five to get prefix had the letter above the number. These were Nos.E9458 (12th), E9482 (20th), E9469 (27th), all February 1948; E9446 (5th) and E9431 (10th), both March 1948.

4603 cont./
Don. 26/7—20/11/26.**G.**
Don. 16/2—6/4/29.**G.**
Don. 9/5—6/6/31.**G.**
Don. 16/11—14/12/35.**G.**
Don. 30/4—14/5/38.**G.**
Don. 17/8—7/9/40.**G.**
Don. 2—23/10/43.**G.**
Don. 20/1—10/2/45.**G.**
Don. 6/10—10/11/45.**G.**
Don. 23/9—28/10/47.**G.**
Don. 2—27/1/50.**G.**
Str. 6/4—21/5/52.**G.**
Don. 8/2/55. *Not repaired.*

BOILERS:
7149.
7676 *(Sup.)* 23/2/24.
8404 14/12/35.
8834 7/9/40.
9257 28/10/47.
8540 27/1/50.
21513 21/5/52.

SHEDS:
King's Cross.
Bradford 12/11/26.
Hatfield 16/10/39.
Bradford 5/3/44.
Copley Hill 18/2/51.

RENUMBERED:
4603 23/2/24.
9483 7/7/46.
69483 27/1/50.

CONDEMNED: 7/3/55.
Cut up at Doncaster.

———————————————

4604

Doncaster 1349.

To traffic 6/1912.

REPAIRS:
Don. 4/10/22—16/2/23.**G.**
*In GNR green but lettered
L&NER.*
Don. 31/7—7/11/25.**G.**
Don. 19/11/27—10/2/28.**G.**
Don. 29/3—26/4/30.**G.**
Don. 15/10—5/11/32.**G.**
Don. 13/7—10/8/35.**G.**
Fountain lub. fitted.
Don. 21/1—4/2/39.**G.**
Str. 6/3—26/6/43.**G.**
Don. 9/4—18/6/47.**G.**
Str. 14/8—30/9/50.**G.**
Don. 21/1—19/2/54.**G.**

BOILERS:
7150.
6954 7/11/25.
8390 10/8/35.
7996 26/6/43.
9803 18/6/47.
9803 reno.21474 30/9/50.
21268 19/2/54.

SHEDS:
King's Cross.
Hatfield 4/3/29.
King's Cross 6/10/30.
Hatfield 6/6/48.
Ardsley 23/9/51.

RENUMBERED:
4604 7/11/25.
9484 27/7/46.
69484 30/9/50.

CONDEMNED: 30/9/57.
Cut up at Doncaster.

———————————————

4605

Doncaster 1350.

To traffic 6/1912.

REPAIRS:
Don. 18/10/22—5/3/23.**G.**
Green livery, lettered L&NER.
Don. 19/5—22/8/25.**G.**
Don. 24/9—3/12/27.**G.**
Don. 30/11—31/12/29.**G.**
Don. 16/7—13/8/32.**G.**
Don. 13/7—3/8/35.**G.**
Fountain lub. for horncheeks.
Str. 13/12/38—27/1/39.**G.**
Don. 6/12/41—17/1/42.**G.**
Don. 29/4—27/5/44.**G.**
Don. 4/8—15/9/45.**G.**
Don. 5—19/1/46.**L.**

Don. 15/1—8/2/47.**L.**
Don. 6/11—16/12/47.**G.**
Don. 9/1—24/2/50.**G.**
Str. 1/2—29/3/52.**G.**
Str. 20/7—21/8/53.**C/L.**
Don. 20/10/54. *Not repaired.*

BOILERS:
7151.
7056 3/12/27.
8734 3/8/35.
7412 27/1/39.
9278 17/1/42.
8528 16/12/47.
21511 29/3/52.

SHEDS:
King's Cross.
Hatfield 15/4/29.
King's Cross 20/6/29.
Hornsey 16/9/32.
King's Cross 7/11/32.
Hatfield 24/4/42.
Bradford 5/11/43.

RENUMBERED:
4605 22/8/25.
9485 27/10/46.
69485 24/2/50.

CONDEMNED: 1/11/54.
Cut up at Doncaster.

———————————————

The next one ex-works No.69456 on 26th April 1948 had full BR number and, still in 12in. figures. Others with 12in. figures were 69449, 69453, 69459, 69468, 69676 (13th May), 69481 (26th May).

E9446 went to Doncaster 22nd September 1948 for a light repair, and when out 22nd October, the 6 had been added to the number and the E had only been thinly obliterated. Wakefield Kirkgate, 30th April 1949.

By early July numbers on bunker had become 10in. instead of 12in. to be more in keeping with the $7^{1}/_{2}$in. lettering, but the 6 and 9 were still the LNER modified Gill sans. Doncaster shed, September 1951.

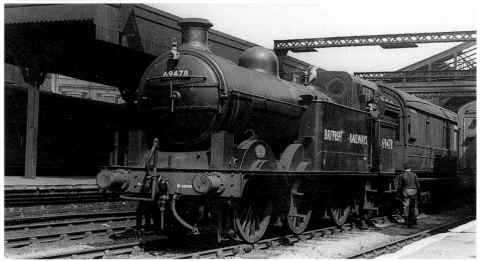

By early 1949 letters and numbers had been made the same 10in. in height and the 6 and 9 were correct Gill sans. Plain black continued to be used despite the change to the emblem which Doncaster put on to 69472 (15th September), 69464 (30th September) and 69474 (19th October), all 1949. Leeds Central, April 1949.

(above) **Beginning with 69450, ex-works 16th December 1949, Doncaster also applied red, cream and grey lining to 69434, 69439, 69440, 69444, 69448, 69459, 69482, 69483, 69485 by 20th June 1950 and then Stratford took over maintenance until the end of 1953.**

(right) **From September 1950 to December 1953 the whole class (including those shedded in the West Riding) were sent to Stratford for repair, and all those ex-works by the end of 1953 were in unlined black. Bradford shed, April 1953.**

No.69440 ex-Doncaster on 17th February 1950 was one of the ten to which BR lining had been applied.

The last two at Stratford went in 1953 but were not ex-works until into 1954. They were 69447 (30th November 1953 to 16th January 1954) and 69464 (9th December 1953 to 13th February 1954). Curiously, they were both given lining and 69447 was an oddity being the only one seen with a rail on the smokebox door above the number plate. Stratford shed.

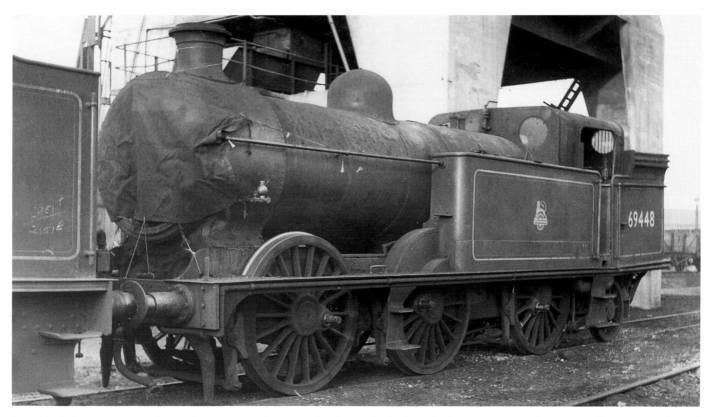

69448 had lining put on by Doncaster 24th March 1950 and this survived a Stratford general repair from which it was ex-works 2nd August 1952. Working from Bradford shed it suffered this mishap and was sent into Doncaster works on 8th December 1952. They simply sent it on to Stratford, which is how this 14th December 1952 photograph was taken at Cambridge. Stratford did not repair it and it as withdrawn on 12th January 1953.

Maintenance by Doncaster was resumed when 69484 went in there on 21st January 1954 and by August 1956, twelve N1's, 69430, 69434, 69443, 69449, 69450, 69452, 69453, 69462, 69472, 69474, 69477 and 69484 had been given a general repair. Only two of them 69430 (2nd April 1954) and 69477 (9th June 1956) had lining put on. Doncaster shed, 17th June 1956.

No.69452 was out 13th April 1956 from its last repair, still superheated and in plain black. Withdrawn 13th March 1959, it was still intact - apart from safety valves - on Doncaster scrap road 12th April 1959. The withdrawal of 69462 on 3rd April 1959 made the N1 class extinct for traffic purposes. None changed from the emblem to the 1957 crest.

On 27th May 1954 No.69461 arrived at Stratford from Ardsley but it was not repaired and on the 7th June was withdrawn from traffic. In November 1954 Stratford made it their Stationery Boiler No.3294 and installed it at Shoeburyness for pre-heating coaches. It served on that duty until December 1962 and by 21st January 1963 SB 3294 was back at Stratford and it was cut up during March. Shoeburyness, 10th September 1955.

(left) **Thirty more engines of the same type, Nos.1721 to 1750, were built by the North British Locomotive Co., Glasgow, from December 1920 to February 1921. These engines had a handrail fitted on the side of the tank and this was kept to withdrawal, but only these thirty were so fitted. King's Cross shed, April 1921.**

(above) **Another twenty engines which completed the N.B.Loco. order, Nos.1751 to 1770, were delivered during March and April 1921; these did not have a rail on the side of the tank. The sixty engines all had right hand drive, condensing apparatus, were to Metropolitan Railway load gauge and, constituted Part 1 of the class. King's Cross shed.**

(left) **Nos.2583 to 2594 were built by Beyer, Peacock, Manchester in February and March 1925. They had left hand drive and a taller chimney, all twelve being for the Scottish Area and they became Part 2 of the class. Condensing apparatus was not required on them. No.2589 is seen at York on its delivery run to Scotland.**

CLASS N 2

4606

Doncaster 1518.

To traffic 12/1920.

REPAIRS:
Don. 6/6—29/9/23.**G.**
Don. 2/7—15/8/25.**G.**
Don. 12/10—9/12/27.**G.**
Don. 20/7—29/8/29.**G.**
Don. 26/6—24/8/31.**G.**
Don. 18/8—9/10/33.**G.**
Don. 9/8—3/10/35.**G.**
Don. 30/6—4/8/37.**G.**
Don. 4/6—1/7/39.**G.**
Str. 10/1—18/5/43.**G.**
Don. 9/11/45—4/1/46.**L.**
Don. 11/2—20/3/46.**G.**
Don. 29/5—8/7/48.**G.**
Don. 18/8—29/9/50.**G.**
Don. 23/3—21/4/53.**G.**
Don. 14—20/5/53.**N/C.**
Str. 8/9—20/10/55.**G.**

BOILERS:
7537.
7589 29/8/29.
9141 1/7/39.
9177 18/5/43.
21204 29/9/50.
21404 21/4/53.
21347 20/10/55.

SHED:
King's Cross.

RENUMBERED:
1606ɴ 29/9/23.
4606 15/8/25.
9490 28/9/46.
69490 8/7/48.

CONDEMNED: 6/7/59.
Into Don. for cut up 6/7/59.

4607

Doncaster 1519.

To traffic 4/1921.

REPAIRS:
Don. 1/4—17/5/24.**G.**
Don. 8/2—28/4/26.**G.**
Don. 14/7—5/9/28.**G.**
Don. 2/4—23/5/30.**G.**
Don. 6/11/31—16/1/32.**G.**
Don. 30/6—5/9/33.**G.**
Don. 19/7—29/8/35.**G.**

Don. 2/9—4/10/37.**G.**
Don. 11/12/38—16/2/39.**G.**
Don. 25/4—27/5/41.**G.**
Don. 13/5—15/6/44.**G.**
Don. 30/4—15/6/46.**G.**
Don. 9/3—22/4/48.**G.**
Don. 5/10—3/11/50.**G.**
Don. 7/5—5/6/53.**G.**
Str. 19/9—10/11/55.**G.**
Str. 5—8/12/55.**N/C.**
Don. 22/1/59.*Not repaired.*

BOILERS:
7536.
7578 16/1/32.
7540 29/8/35.
7539 15/6/44.
8936 22/4/48.
21220 3/11/50.
21222 5/6/53.
21456 10/11/55.

SHEDS:
King's Cross.
Ardsley 25/4/26.
King's Cross 11/12/26.

RENUMBERED:
4607 17/5/24.
9491 24/2/46.
69491 22/4/48.

CONDEMNED: 26/1/59.
Cut up at Doncaster.

4608

Doncaster 1521.

To traffic 5/1921.

REPAIRS:
Don. 1/4—17/5/24.**G.**
Don. 27/4—30/8/26.**G.**
Don. 11/6—24/8/28.**G.**
Don. 15/9—13/11/30.**G.**
Don. 13/8—19/10/32.**G.**
Don. 28/7—18/9/34.**G.**
Don. 30/7—27/8/36.**G.**
Str. 24/4—2/6/38.**G.**
T.A.B. valves fitted.
Str. 26/3—6/4/39.**L.**
Don. 21/11/40—4/1/41.**G.**
Don. 27/12/43—27/1/44.**G.**
Don. 17/3—10/5/47.**G.**
Don. 30/1—30/3/50.**G.**
Don. 29/8—10/10/51.**C/L.**
Don. 31/8—3/10/52.**G.**
Don. 29/12/53—25/1/54.**C/L.**
Str. 10/6—4/9/54.**C/L.**

Str. 9/12/54—19/3/55.**C/L.**
Str. 28/2—14/4/56.**C/H.**

BOILERS:
7538.
7536 19/10/32.
7586 2/6/38.
9333 27/1/44.
10557 30/3/50.
21377 3/10/52.
21454 14/4/56.

SHED:
King's Cross.

RENUMBERED:
4608 17/5/24.
9492 26/1/46.
69492 30/3/50.

*CONDEMNED:*26/11/59.
Into Don. for cut up 26/11/59.

4609

Doncaster 1523.

To traffic 6/1921.

REPAIRS:
Don. 17/5—21/6/24.**G.**
Don. 18/1—8/4/27.**G.**
Don. 16/10—15/12/28.**G.**
Don. 26/10/30—16/1/31.**G.**
Don. 20/10—5/12/33.**G.**
Don. 23/1—21/2/36.**G.**
Str. 24/11—30/12/37.**G.**
Don. 11/7—6/8/40.**G.**
Str. 30/10/42—16/2/43.**G.**
Don. 30/7—15/9/45.**G.**
Don. 15/5—26/6/48.**G.**
Str. 17/11—18/12/50.**G.**
Don. 7/3—9/4/53.**G.**
Str. 9/1—29/2/56.**G.**

BOILERS:
7540.
7538 5/12/33.
7575 30/12/37.
7572 6/8/40.
8105 16/2/43.
8818 26/6/48.
21404 *(new)* 18/12/50.
21454 9/4/53.
21395 29/2/56.

SHEDS:
King's Cross.
Hatfield 17/7/49.
King's Cross 2/12/51.

RENUMBERED:
4609 21/6/24.
9493 13/9/46.
69493 26/6/48.

*CONDEMNED:*9/12/58.
Into Don. for cut up 9/12/58.

4610

Doncaster 1524.

To traffic 6/1921.

REPAIRS:
Don. 17/4—31/5/24.**G.**
Don. 5/7—9/10/26.**G.**
Don. 2/8—13/10/28.**G.**
Don. 18/3—24/4/30.**G.**
Don. 28/11/31—18/2/32.**G.**
Don. 1/12/33—14/2/34.**G.**
Don. 10/3—16/4/36.**G.**
Str. 5/11—17/12/37.**G.**
Don. 14/6—12/8/39.**G.**
Str. 10/11/42—28/4/43.**G.**
Don. 16/1—23/2/46.**G.**
Don. 15/8—11/10/48.**G.**
Don. 6/2—1/3/50.**C/L.**
Don. 11/3—6/4/51.**G.**
Str. 12/1—18/2/54.**N/C.**
Str. 30/1—12/3/55.**G.**
Str. 1/12/57. *Not repaired*

BOILERS:
7541.
7575 14/2/34.
C1682 17/12/37.
9177 12/8/39.
9141 28/4/43.
8283 11/10/48.
21259 6/4/51.
21362 12/3/55.

SHEDS:
King's Cross.
Hatfield 11/6/50.
Grantham 26/8/51.
King's Cross 9/9/51.
Hatfield 2/12/51.
King's Cross 22/8/54.
Hatfield 19/9/54.

RENUMBERED:
4610 31/5/24.
9494 17/3/46.
69494 9/10/48.

*CONDEMNED:*13/1/58.
Cut up at Stratford.

(left) As delivered to Scotland they had the usual two coal rails (see previous illustration) but the top one was quickly taken off as being too high for their coal stages. They also differed from Part 1 in being fitted with destination board clips at the top of the smokebox front instead of brackets on the door. Eastfield, June 1928.

(opposite, top) Yorkshire Engine Co., Sheffield, were given an order for nine and the first three, Nos.2682 to 2684 were for London District so were to Metropolitan gauge. These had condensing apparatus and were also Part 4, being delivered from 25th September to 2nd November 1928.

Six more for Scottish Area, Nos.892 to 897 were built at Doncaster in November and December 1925. Their coupled wheel journals were 8¼in. x 8in. instead of 7½in. x 7in., with deeper frames. They had Westinghouse brakes for engine and train with vacuum ejector, so became Part 3.

Twenty more N2's, Nos.2662 to 2681, were built by Hawthorn, Leslie & Co. Newcastle, from September 1928 to April 1929, all to Metropolitan gauge and fitted with GER pattern condensing apparatus. They had a deeper ashpan to provide a door at the back and their boiler had Ross 'pop' safety valves. Buffers were Group Standard type and leading sanders were gravity instead of steam operated. They were given Part 4.

The other six, Nos.2685 to 2690, were delivered from Yorkshire Engine Co. between 22nd December 1928 and 20th March 1929. They were destined for Scottish Area so had 16³/₈ in. chimney, no condensing gear, but still went with two coal rails. Although only vacuum braked, they were added to Part 3. Doncaster works, on delivery.

On the first sixty engines the condensate drain pipe at the smokebox bend was only a half inch in diameter and by November 1921 had proved too small, so was replaced by one which was an inch in diameter. These pipes passed behind the sandbox to discharge on to the track (*see* page 47, bottom).

4611

Doncaster 1525.

To traffic 7/1921.

REPAIRS:
Don. 1/4—24/5/24.**G.**
Don. 1/7—28/10/26.**G.**
Don. 29/12/28—21/2/29.**G.**
Don. 24/1—1/4/31.**G.**
Don. 22/10—22/12/32.**G.**
Don. 3/5—15/6/35.**G.**
Str. 3/1—19/3/37.**G.**
Str. 27/4—16/6/39.**G.**
Don. 5/1—3/3/42.**G.**
Don. 7—28/10/44.**G.**
Don. 9/7—18/9/47.**G.**
Don. 3—28/7/50.**G.**
Don. 12/12/52—9/1/53.**G.**
Str. 15/4—21/5/55.**G.**

BOILERS:
7539.
8282 1/4/31.
7679 19/3/37.
7584 16/6/39.
9325 3/3/42.
8396 28/10/44.
8986 28/7/50.
21395 9/1/53.
21411 21/5/55.

SHEDS:
King's Cross.
Doncaster 2/5/42.
Mexborough 9/5/42.
Hatfield 6/12/42.
King's Cross 30/1/44.

RENUMBERED:
4611 24/5/24.
9495 13/9/46.
69495 28/7/50.

*CONDEMNED:*25/9/58.
Into Don. for cut up 25/9/58.

4612

Doncaster 1527.

To traffic 7/1921.

REPAIRS:
Don. 5/5—14/6/24.**G.**
Don. 18/1—6/4/27.**G.**
Don. 15/11/28—1/2/29.**G.**
Don. 29/11/30—17/2/31.**G.**
Don. 17/9—2/12/32.**G.**
Gor. 25/6—11/8/34.**G.**
Str. 5/10—19/11/36.**G.**
Str. 4/8—23/9/38.**G.**
Don. 3/11—11/12/40.**G.**

Don. 17/2—15/3/44.**G.**
Don. 13/1—22/4/47.**G.**
Don. 14/8—16/9/49.**G.**
Don. 16/3—18/4/52.**G.**
Don. 11—20/5/52.**N/C.**
Don. 17/12/52—23/1/53.**C/H.**
Str. 31/1—5/3/55.**G.**
Str. 10/4/58. *Not repaired.*

BOILERS:
7542.
7564 2/12/32.
7563 11/8/34.
7573 19/11/36.
1362 23/9/38.
7574 15/3/44.
9616 22/4/47.
21411 *(new)* 18/4/52.
21415 5/3/55.

SHEDS:
King's Cross.
Neasden 5/11/43.
King's Cross 21/4/44.
Hornsey 29/9/57.
King's Cross 24/11/57.

RENUMBERED:
4612 14/6/24.
9496 11/10/46.
69496 16/9/49.

*CONDEMNED:*14/4/58.
Cut up at Stratford.

4613

Doncaster 1528.

To traffic 8/1921.

REPAIRS:
Don. 23/5—28/6/24.**G.**
Don. 16/7—2/8/24.**N/C.**
Don. 3/9—10/12/26.**G.**
Don. 21/10/28—31/1/29.**G.**
Don. 11/6—22/8/30.**G.**
Don. 27/2—17/6/32.**G.**
Don. 9/2—4/5/34.**G.**
Don. 1—31/7/36.**G.**
Str. 25/3—21/5/38.**G.**
Don. 12—29/7/40.**G.**
Don. 27/12/43—27/1/44.**G.**
Don. 3/9—26/10/46.**G.**
Don. 17/4—12/5/49.**G.**
Don. 8/5—6/6/52.**G.**
Str. 27/9—13/11/54.**G.**
Str. 17/12/54—22/1/55.**C/L.**
Don. 16/11—30/11/56.**C/L.**
Don. 11/3/58. *Not repaired.*

BOILERS:
7543.
7586 22/8/30.

7572 21/5/38.
7538 29/7/40.
9140 26/10/46.
21360 6/6/52.
21510 13/11/54.

SHED:
King's Cross.

RENUMBERED:
4613 28/6/24.
9497 26/10/46.
69497 12/5/49.

*CONDEMNED:*17/3/58.
Cut up at Doncaster.

4614

Doncaster 1530.

To traffic 8/1921.

REPAIRS:
Don. 1/4—17/5/24.**G.**
Don. 12/8—16/11/26.**G.**
Don. 13/10—20/12/28.**G.**
Don. 9/2—26/3/31.**G.**
Don. 26/11/32—14/2/33.**G.**
*Rail washing gear and dry
sanding fitted to leading wheels.*
Don. 10/12/34—18/1/35.**G.**
Str. 25/10—4/12/36.**G.**
Don. 14/1—25/3/39.**G.**
Don. 1/7—1/8/41.**G.**
Don. 19/8—9/9/44.**G.**
Don. 30/12/44—12/2/45.**G.**
Don. 6/1—6/2/48.**G.**
Don. 4—26/1/51.**G.**
Don. 11/12/52—19/1/53.**G.**
Str. 15/4—21/5/55.**G.**
Str. 17/1—15/3/58.**G.**

BOILERS:
7544.
8284 26/3/31.
7544 4/12/36.
9144 25/3/39.
8567 6/2/48.
21233 26/1/51.
21398 19/1/53.
21259 21/5/55.
21291 15/3/58.

SHEDS:
King's Cross.
Hornsey 25/9/60.
New England 9/7/61.

RENUMBERED:
4614 17/5/24.
9498 3/2/46.
ᴇ9498 6/2/48.
69498 26/1/51.

CONDEMNED: 11/9/61.
Into Don. for cut up 11/9/61.

4615

Doncaster 1531.

To traffic 8/1921.

REPAIRS:
Don. 30/1—8/3/22.**L.**
Don. 30/5—12/7/24.**G.**
Don. 8/1—1/4/27.**G.**
Don. 29/9—30/11/28.**G.**
Don. 2/5—27/6/30.**G.**
Don. 30/4—31/8/32.**G.**
Gor. 21/7—22/9/34.**G.**
Don. 2/7—4/8/36.**G.**
Str. 26/8—12/10/38.**G.**
Str. 21/2—29/4/39.**L.**
Don. 3/5—7/6/41.**G.**
Don. 6/6—8/7/44.**G.**
Don. 29/1—3/3/45.**L.**
Str. 10/12/46—15/2/47.**G.**
Don. 6/9—21/10/49.**G.**
Don. 21/5—18/6/52.**G.**
Str. 31/12/54—19/2/55.**G.**
Str. 18—22/3/55.**N/C.**
Don. 11/9/58. *Not repaired.*

BOILERS:
7545.
7575 27/6/30.
7573 31/8/32.
7564 22/9/34.
8993 12/10/38.
8814 15/2/47.
21362 18/6/52.
21282 19/2/55.

SHEDS:
King's Cross.
Hornsey 16/9/32.
King's Cross 7/11/32.

RENUMBERED:
4615 12/7/24.
9499 8/12/46.
69499 21/10/49.

*CONDEMNED:*15/9/58.
Cut up at Doncaster.

4721

N.B. Loco. 22577.

To traffic 12/1920.

REPAIRS:
Don. 31/8—3/11/23.**G.**
Don. 2/7—15/8/25.**G.**
Don. 17/5—22/7/27.**G.**

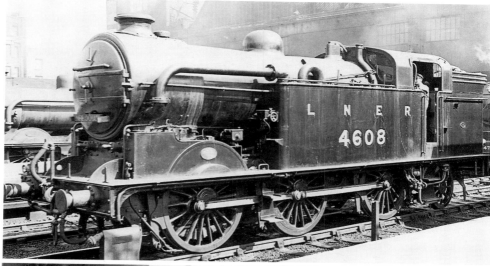

Beginning with No.4610 ex-works 9th October 1926, the 1in. pipe was altered to pass down the front of the sandbox and all were so changed at their next works visit. King's Cross station, June 1938.

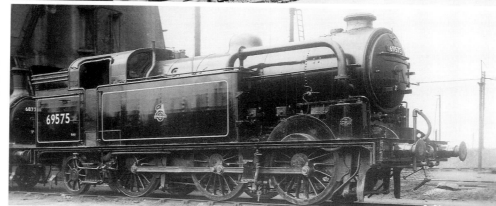

The later built engines fitted for condensing had the 1926 drain pipe arrangement which was kept to withdrawal.

The sixty built for the GNR did not have the handrails along the sides and across the back of the bunker. An instruction was issued in April 1924 for this rail to be added and all sixty were then so equipped. However, No.4747 ex-works 3rd May 1924, was still without this rail.

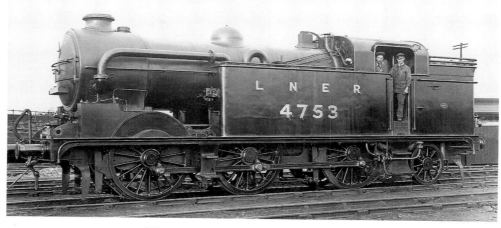

Lubrication of coupled wheel axleboxes was by ordinary siphon trimming feed. Although designed for suburban passenger work, the N2's did some branch line goods jobs, so a few acquired GNR load Class F collar on their vacuum standpipe. None appear to have carried LNER load Class 2, introduced in July 1924 for Southern area.

Ex-works 9th September 1922, No.1736 had been changed to a No.7 Wakefield mechanical lubricator for the axleboxes, mounted on the left hand side, just behind the leading splasher. This proved more effective and reduced oil consumption by about a pint a day. On 12th June 1925 five more were authorised and then, from 17th December 1925, all were to be so fitted. Doncaster works.

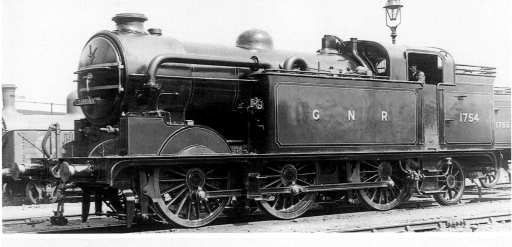

The Wakefield No.7 mechanical lubricator mounted on the front end of the left hand tank served cylinders and steam chest. Its anti-carboniser at first took superheated steam from the header inside the smokebox.

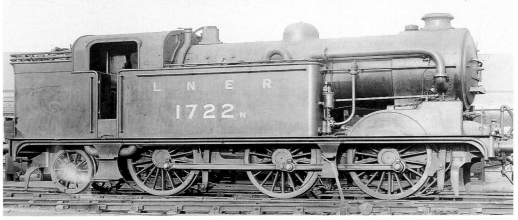

The superheated steam gave trouble, so from 1923 - No.1722N was ex-works 6th October 1923 - the anti-carboniser was fed with saturated steam taken from the blower valve on the right hand side.

The original intention was to have the handrail along the side of the tank below the top edge and Nos.1721 to 1730 arrived from N.B. Loco Co. so fitted. Meanwhile, Doncaster had changed the position of the rail and placed it on top of the tank (see illustration in the Introduction).

4721 cont./
Cow. 10/10/27—?/1/28.**G.**
Westinghouse brake added.
(Cowlairs records missing).
Cow. ?/11—?/12/32.**G.**
Cow. ?/?—15/12/34.**G.**
Cow. 28/12/35—?/2/36.**H.**
Cow. ?/?—12/11/36.**G.**
Cow. ?/?—?/1/37.**L.**
Cow. ?/?—17/3/38.**L.**
Cow. ?/4—13/5/39.**G.**
Cow. ?/?—1/12/42.**L.**
Cow. 22/7—26/8/44.**G.**
Cow. 19—26/10/46.**L.**
Westinghouse brake removed.
Cow. 30—31/10/47.**L.**
Cow. 24/8—28/9/48.**G.**
Cow. ?/?—3/2/50.**C/L.**
Cow. 30/7—25/8/51.**G.**
Inv. 23/11—18/12/53.**L/I.**
Cow. 24/5—1/6/54.**N/C.**
Cow. 22/11—11/12/54.**C/H.**

BOILERS:
7551.
7682 22/7/27.
7682 reno.C1663 ?/?/?.
8134 (exDon.) 13/5/39.
C1671 (ex4735) 26/8/44.
21545 (ex9564) 25/8/51.
21547 (ex69564) 11/12/54.

SHEDS:
King's Cross.
Scotland 31/7/27.
Parkhead 10/8/27.
Carlisle Canal ?/12/38.
Bathgate ?/9/42.
Carlisle Canal 12/12/43.
Kipps 19/3/45.
Bathgate 21/5/45.
Parkhead 19/1/47.

RENUMBERED:
1721N 3/11/23.
4721 2/3/25.
9500 31/3/46.
69500 28/9/48.

CONDEMNED: 1/8/57.
Cut up at Cowlairs 8/57.

4722

N.B. Loco. 22578.

To traffic 12/1920.

REPAIRS:
Don. 11/7—6/10/23.**G.**

Don. 14/10—5/12/25.**G.**
Don. 18/5—6/8/27.**G.**
Cow. 10/10/27—?/?/?.**?.**
Cow. 25/1—6/2/28.**N/C.**
Dual brake fitted.
Cow. 12—25/9/28.**L.**
Cow. 27/11/29—15/2/30.**G.**
Back ashpan damper fitted.
Cow. 9/12/31—2/2/32.**G.**
Str. 24/5—15/6/32.**L.**
Str. 5/1—24/2/33.**H.**
Str. 19/3—20/5/35.**G.**
Str. 14/9—19/10/37.**G.**
Str. 20/2—21/2/40.**N/C.**
Westinghouse pump removed.
Don. 4/1—4/4/41.**G.**
Don. 4/5—11/6/43.**G.**
Don. 25/6—16/8/47.**G.**
Don. 8/11—8/12/50.**G.**
Str. 19/8—25/9/54.**G.**
Str. 5—11/10/54.**N/C.**

BOILERS:
7552.
7678 6/8/27.
7556 20/5/35.
7598 19/10/37.
9226 4/4/41.
21402 (new) 8/12/50.
21529 25/9/54.

SHEDS:
King's Cross.
Dundee 10/8/27.
Stratford 3/2/32.
Hatfield 22/2/40.
Doncaster 12/10/42.
Mexborough 18/6/44.
Hatfield 4/11/45.
Colwick 10/11/47.
Hatfield 6/5/51.
Grantham 26/8/51.
Hatfield 9/9/51.
King's Cross 27/9/53.
Hornsey 14/2/54.

RENUMBERED:
1722N 6/10/23.
4722 ?/4/25 (at shed).
9501 14/4/46.
69501 8/12/50.

CONDEMNED: 20/11/57.
Into Don. for cut up 20/11/57.

4723

N.B. Loco. 22579.

To traffic 12/1920.

REPAIRS:
Don. 8—23/12/22.**L.**
Don. 31/8—20/11/23.**G.**
Don. 23/10—12/12/25.**G.**
Don. 6/7—28/9/27.**G.**
Cow. 7/10—5/12/27.**L.**
Cow. 2/2—3/3/28.**N/C.**
For Dual fitting.
Cow. 24/5—19/9/28.**N/C.**
For inspection.
Cow. 30/7—3/8/29.**G.**
Cow. 16/7—30/8/30.**G.**
Cow. 22/3—23/4/32.**G.**
Str. 27/5—15/6/32.**N/C.**
Str. 5/1—17/2/33.**H.**
Str. 23/3—7/6/35.**G.**
Str. 7—31/12/37.**L.**
Str. 23/12/38—17/3/39.**G.**
Westinghouse brake removed.
Don. 4/10—23/11/41.**G.**
Don. 18/7—19/8/44.**G.**
Don. 25/1—8/3/46.**G.**
Don. 29/10—5/12/47.**G.**
Don. 19/7—17/8/50.**G.**
Don. 4/2—25/3/53.**C/L.**
Str. 8/12/53—6/2/54.**G.**
Str. 23/6—27/8/55.**C/L.**
Don. 9/5/58. *Not repaired.*

BOILERS:
7553.
7595 7/6/35.
7553 17/3/39.
8715 19/8/44.
9480 17/8/50.
9480 reno.21453 25/3/53.
21288 6/2/54.

SHEDS:
King's Cross.
Scotland 7/10/27.
Dunfermline 6/12/27.
Parkhead 3/3/28.
Stratford 28/4/32.
Hatfield 17/3/39.
Doncaster 3/10/42.
Mexborough 18/6/44.
Doncaster 17/9/44.
Mexborough 15/3/45.
Hatfield 4/11/45.
King's Cross 23/2/48.
Grantham 26/8/51.
King's Cross 9/9/51.
Stratford 13/7/52.
Parkeston 3/8/52.
King's Cross 28/10/56.
Hornsey 21/4/57.

RENUMBERED:
1723N 20/11/23.
4723 2/3/25.

9502 24/3/46.
69502 17/8/50.

*CONDEMNED:*12/5/58.
Cut up at Doncaster.

4724

N.B. Loco. 22580.

To traffic 12/1920.

REPAIRS:
Don. 5/9—10/11/23.**G.**
Don. 7/11—5/12/25.**G.**
Don. 17/5—16/7/27.**G.**
Cow. 10/10/27—?/1/28.**N/C.**
Westinghouse brake fitted.
(Cowlairs records missing).
Cow. ?/?—21/4/34.**G.**
Cow. ?/?—1/8/34.**L.**
Cow. ?/?—?/2/36.**L.**
Cow. ?/?—11/6/36.**G.**
Cow. ?/?—21/8/36.**L.**
Cow. 25/2—18/3/39.**G.**
Cow. 23/11—21/12/40.**H.**
Cow. ?/?—14/6/45.**L.**
Cow. 9/2—31/3/46.**G.**
Westinghouse brake removed.
Cow. 30/8—6/9/47.**L.**
Cow. 7/4—7/8/48.**G.**
Cow. ?/?—15/4/49.**C/L.**
Cow. 25/9—27/10/51.**G.**
Cow. 25/8—3/9/52.**C/L.**
Cow. 6—9/7/53.**N/C.**
Inv. 8/4—28/5/55.**C/H.**
Not in use 226 days in 1944.

BOILERS:
7554.
7554 reno.C1666 ?/?/?.
C1670 (ex4728) 21/4/34.
C1674 (ex4732) 18/3/39.
C1666 (ex4735) 21/12/40.
7582 (ex4732) 31/3/46.
21536 (ex69514) 27/10/51.

SHEDS:
King's Cross.
Scotland 1/8/27.
Dunfermline 6/12/27.
Carlisle Canal *after 28/2/31;*
probably 6/31.
Darlington 29/1/42.
Carlisle Canal 27/5/42.
Kipps 19/3/45.
Aberdeen Ferryhill 10/6/54.

RENUMBERED:
1724N 10/11/23.

WORKS CODES:- Bpk - Beyer, Peacock. Cw - Cowlairs. Dar- Darlington. Don - Doncaster. Ghd - Gateshead. Gor - Gorton. Inv - Inverurie. Str - Stratford.
REPAIR CODES:- **C/H** - Casual Heavy. **C/L** - Casual Light. **G** - General. **H**- Heavy. **H/I** - Heavy Intermediate. **L** - Light. **L/I** - Light Intermediate. **N/C** - Non-Classified.

49

NORTH BRITISH LOCOMOTIVE COMPANY, LIMITED, GLASGOW.

No.1731 onwards had the rail on top of the tank but to No.1750 there was also a rail on the side of the tank. Note the two extra coal rails across the back of the bunker. But it is unlikely that any were sent to Doncaster so fitted.

For this Engine, quote Reference No. L734 or Code Word ARISBLANCO.
Gauge of Railway, 4-ft. 8½-in.

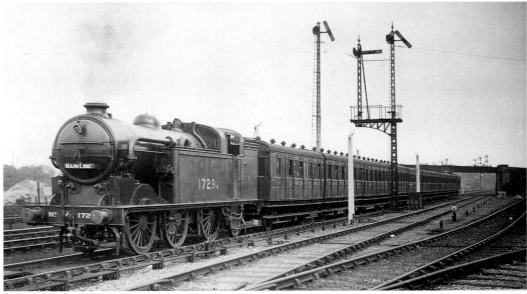

(above) Nos.1751 to 1770 were then delivered with just the one rail - on the tank top - just like Doncaster had turned out Nos.1606 to 1615. King's Cross shed.

(left) Although Nos.1721 to 1730 had arrived with only a rail on the side of the tank, Doncaster left these in place but quickly fitted them also with a tank top rail, so thirty had two rails and the other thirty had one. The thirty with the extra rail became LNER 4721 to 4750 and BR 69500 to 69529. They retained both rails to withdrawal as can still be seen on the preserved engine No.4744. Wood Green.

Between 1st August 1927 and 22nd August 1928, Nos.4721 to 4740 were transferred to Scottish Area and Cowlairs quickly removed the condensing apparatus, as this was not needed in Scotland.

Delivery of Class V1 made it possible for the Scottish Area to return Nos.4725, 4727, 4730, 4733, 4734 and 4738 to London District between 24th September 1930 and 22nd September 1931. All were quickly refitted at Doncaster with condensing apparatus and trip cock gear. 4725 was actually allocated to Doncaster shed from 8th June to 22nd September 1931.

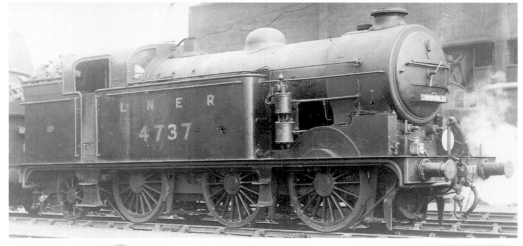

Seven others were also returned to London District, Nos.4722, 4723, 4726, 4731, 4732, 4737 and 4740. No.4737 had returned on 9th May 1929 whilst the others arrived between 4th January and 9th May 1932. Because they had been fitted by Cowlairs with Westinghouse brake, they went to Stratford shed and did not regain condensing apparatus or trip cock gear. Stratford shed.

Nos.2583 to 2594 were the first to have left hand drive and when working in Scotland did not have - or need - condensing apparatus. Note only one coal rail now fitted. Craigentenny.

4724 16/3/25.
9503 31/3/46.
69503 7/8/48.

*CONDEMNED:*3/1/57.
Cut up at Kilmarnock 3/57.

4725

N.B. Loco. 22581.

To traffic 12/1920.

REPAIRS:
Don. 8/1—14/2/24.**G.**
Don. 7/11/25—16/1/26.**G.**
Don. 8/7—8/10/27.**G.**
Cow. ?/?—26/11/27.**L.**
Cow. 22/6—23/8/29.**G.**
Cow. 7/5—8/6/31.**G.**
Don. 15/8—22/9/31.**L.**
Condensing gear refitted.
Don. 5/1—17/2/33.**G.**
Gor. 12/10—15/12/34.**G.**
Gor. 20/12/34—25/1/35.**L.**
Str. 1/1—8/3/37.**G.**
Str. 1/4—31/5/39.**G.**
Str. 26/4—18/6/42.**G.**
Str. 25/6—2/7/42.**N/C.**
Don. 30/11—29/12/44.**G.**
Don. 26/7—1/9/45.**L.**
Don. 1/1—6/2/48.**G.**
Don. 30/4—2/6/50.**G.**
Don. 21/5—18/6/53.**G.**
Don. 10/8—27/9/56.**G.**
Don. 29/1—5/3/59.**G.**

BOILERS:
7555.
7561 17/2/33.
7599 8/3/37.
7560 31/5/39.
8541 6/2/48.
8994 2/6/50.
21401 18/6/53.
21408 27/9/56.
21417 5/3/59.

SHEDS:
King's Cross.
Scotland 6/10/27.
St Margarets 26/11/27.
Doncaster 8/6/31.
King's Cross 22/9/31.
Hatfield 23/2/48.
King's Cross 12/7/53.
Hatfield 27/9/53.
King's Cross 14/3/54.
Hatfield 21/3/54.
King's Cross 25/4/54.
Hatfield 1/8/54.
King's Cross 18/5/58.
Hornsey 15/11/59.
New England 2/7/61.

RENUMBERED:
4725 14/2/24.
9504 24/3/46.
E9504 6/2/48.
69504 2/6/50.

CONDEMNED: 23/9/62.
Into Don. for cut up 15/2/63.

4726

N.B. Loco. 22582.

To traffic 12/1920.

REPAIRS:
Don. 7/1—2/2/24.**G.**
Don. 30/9—14/11/25.**G.**
Don. 18/5—22/7/27.**G.**
Cow. 12/8/27—12/1/28.**N/C.**
Westinghouse brake fitted.
Cow. 3/11/29—11/1/30.**G.**
Cow. 26/2—17/3/30.**L.**
Wheel flange damage.
Cow. 28/8—13/9/30.**L.**
Cow. 13/1—22/2/32.**G.**
Str. 23/2—26/4/33.**H.**
Str. 5/1—25/3/35.**G.**
Str. 12/6—12/8/36.**G.**
Str. 3/1—2/3/39.**G.**
Westinghouse brake removed.
Don. 31/7—6/9/41.**G.**
Don. 3/8—2/9/44.**G.**
Don. 24/12/46—8/2/47.**G.**
Don. 14/2—14/4/50.**G.**
Don. 2/4—1/5/53.**G.**
Don. 29/5—7/7/56.**G.**

BOILERS:
7556.
7541 25/3/35.
7553 12/8/36.
8284 2/3/39.
1373 6/9/41.
8278 8/2/47.
10560 14/4/50.
21215 1/5/53.
21427 *(new)* 7/7/56.

SHEDS:
King's Cross.
Scotland 1/8/27.
Parkhead 12/1/28.
Stratford 22/2/32.
King's Cross 2/3/39.
Hatfield 5/3/39.
Doncaster 18/6/42.
Mexborough 6/8/42.
Hornsey 1/4/46.
Grantham 14/6/59.

RENUMBERED:
1726N 2/2/24.
4726 12/2/25.

9505 28/4/46.
69505 14/4/50.

CONDEMNED: 10/11/60.
Into Don. for cut up 10/11/60.

4727

N.B. Loco. 22583.

To traffic 1/1921.

REPAIRS:
Don. 18/1—23/2/24.**G.**
Don. 11/11/25—16/1/26.**G.**
Don. 8/7—1/10/27.**G.**
Cow. 15/8—5/9/28.**L.**
Firebox mouth cracked.
Cow. 22—24/10/28.**N/C.**
Cow. 10/6—11/7/29.**L.**
Wheel flanges.
Cow. 24/8—18/9/31.**G.**
Ghd. 9—16/10/31.**N/C.**
Don. 20/10—23/11/31.**H.**
Don. 12/5—9/8/33.**G.**
Don. 2/3—9/4/35.**G.**
Str. 30/12/36—12/2/37.**G.**
Str. 29/10—21/12/38.**G.**
Don. 14/4—1/6/40.**G.**
Don. 28/7—28/8/43.**G.**
Don. 18/1—16/3/46.**G.**
Don. 2/10—12/11/48.**G.**
Don. 7/4—2/5/51.**G.**
Don. 9/11—9/12/53.**G.**
Str. 15/9—1/10/55.**N/C.**
Don. 9/11—15/12/56.**G.**
Don. 19—22/12/56.**N/C.**

BOILERS:
7557.
7567 23/11/31.
7543 12/2/37.
7564 21/12/38.
1371 1/6/40.
9065 12/11/48.
21272 2/5/51.
21278 9/12/53.
21312 22/12/56.

SHEDS:
King's Cross.
Scotland 7/10/27.
St Margarets 26/11/27.
King's Cross 18/9/31.
New England 24/1/60.

RENUMBERED:
4727 23/2/24.
9506 31/3/46.
69506 12/11/48.

*CONDEMNED:*31/5/61.
Into Don. for cut up 31/5/61.

4728

N.B. Loco. 22584.

To traffic 1/1921.

REPAIRS:
Don. 19/4—5/5/23.**L.**
Don. 18/1—2/2/24.**G.**
Don. 14/12/25—30/1/26.**G.**
Don. 21/9—17/12/27.**G.**
Westinghouse brake fitted.
(Cowlairs records missing).
Cow. ?/?—21/5/31.**G.**
Cow. 31/3—3/5/34.**G.**
Cow. ?/?—20/2/36.**G.**
Cow. ?/?—14/4/36.**L.**
Cow. ?/?—12/9/38.**G.**
Cow. 14/6—26/7/41.**G.**
Cow. ?/?—29/1/44.**G.**
Cow. 3—10/2/45.**L.**
Cow. 19—26/5/45.**L.**
Cow. 10—30/11/45.**L.**
Westinghouse brake removed.
Cow. 31/10—4/12/47.**G.**
Cow. 4—28/1/50.**H/I.**
Cow. 23—27/4/51.**N/C.**
Cow. 29/4—1/5/52.**N/C.**
Cow. 2—11/6/52.**C/L.**
Cow. 18/11—26/12/52.**G.**
Cow. 12—19/10/53.**C/L.**
Cow. 1—19/3/55.**H/I.**
Cow. 18/10—12/11/55.**C/H.**
Cow. 31/7—24/8/57.**H/I.**

BOILERS:
7558.
7558 reno. C1670 ?/?/?.
C1708 *(ex2690)* 3/5/34.
C1674 *(ex4724)* 26/7/41.
21540 *(ex69562)* 26/12/52.
21539 *(ex69563)* 12/11/55.

SHEDS:
King's Cross.
Neasden 25/4/26.
King's Cross 27/1/27.
Scotland 4/1/28.
Parkhead *by* 12/5/28.
Carlisle Canal ?/12/38.
Parkhead ?/5/41.
Kipps 23/9/51.
Parkhead 14/4/52.

RENUMBERED:
4728 2/2/24.
9507 31/3/46.
69507 28/1/50.

CONDEMNED: 22/4/60.
Cut up at Cowlairs 4/6/60.

(above) New V1 class engines displaced No.2589 to Hatfield on 8th December 1930 and No.2588 to King's Cross shed on 29th December 1931. To make them useful in London District, Doncaster changed their 16³⁄₈ in. chimney to 12³⁄₈ in. pattern and fitted them with condensing apparatus in 1932; No.2588 on 1st March and 2589 on 16th August. No.2586 went to Hatfield on 12th March 1931 and the GE Section from 20th January to 26th April 1932. It then went back to Hatfield until 18th November when permanent transfer to Scottish Area took effect, as it remained unaltered.

(centre) The other nine Part 2 engines were transferred from 5th February 1931 to 26th January 1932 and went to Ardsley and Bradford where they needed no change. On these Part 2 engines the axlebox lubrication was by a No.6 Hulburd mechanical lubricator mounted on the front of the right hand tank. Bradford, 24th May 1931.

(right) On Part 2 engines the cylinder lubrication was not mechanical but was from a Detroit sight feed lubricator in the cab.

(left) Nos.892 to 897 had mechanical lubricator for axleboxes on the front of the right hand tank but it was a Wakefield No.7. Cylinder lubrication was by sight feed in the cab, and that was also of Wakefield manufacture.

The sight feed lubrication on Parts 2 and 3 was split between both sides of the engine.

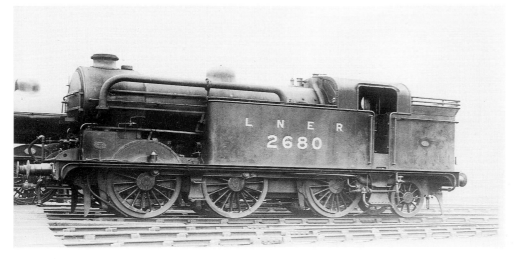

In 1927, trouble when condensing on the first sixty engines was still being caused by water surging back through the pipes. New engines Nos.2662 to 2681 from Hawthorn, Leslie were tried with the GE method of having no U-bend and the pipe into the tank entering about mid-way.

4729

N.B. Loco. 22585.

To traffic 1/1921

REPAIRS:
Don. 4—25/11/22.**L.**
Don. 5/1—19/1/24.**G.**
Don. 9—28/6/24.**L.**
Don. 8/2—29/5/26.**G.**
Don. 4/8—21/10/27.**G.**
Cow. ?/?—?/6/28.**N/C.**
Westinghouse brake fitted.
(Cowlairs records missing).
Cow. 7—31/12/32.**G.**
Cow. ?/?—?/11/33.**L.**
Cow. ?/?—26/10/34.**G.**
Cow. ?/?—27/4/37.**G.**
Cow. 18/11—30/12/39.**G.**
Don. 26/7—16/8/41.**G.**
Cow. ?/?—4/3/44.**G.**
Cow. 28/5—21/6/46.**G.**
Westinghouse brake removed.
Cow. 16—18/10/47.**L.**
Cow. 15/3—17/4/48.**G.**
Cow. 9—28/6/52.**G.**
Cow. 12—19/9/52.**N/C.**
Cow. 26/9—7/10/52.**C/L.**
Cow. 5—13/10/53.**C/L.**
Cow. 30/8—18/9/54.**L/I.**
Cow. 20/9—6/10/55.**N/C.**

BOILERS:
7559.
7559 reno. C1671 ?/?/27.
7417 (ex4739) 30/12/39.
7542 16/8/41.
C1677 (ex893) 21/6/46.
21533 (ex69500) 28/6/52.

SHEDS:
King's Cross.
Scotland 27/10/27.
St Margarets 26/11/27.
Kipps ?/6/33.
Hawick ?/11/35.
St Margarets ?/2/36.
Eastfield ?/10/38.
Stratford 21/1/41.
Eastfield 1/10/41.
Kipps ?/6/44.
Parkhead 23/9/51.

RENUMBERED:
1729ɴ 19/1/24.
4729 late 1/25 (at shed).
9508 31/3/46.
69508 17/4/48.

CONDEMNED: 3/12/59
Cut up at Cowlairs 27/2/60.

4730

N.B. Loco. 22586.

To traffic 1/1921.

REPAIRS:
Don. 2—20/5/22.**L.**
Don. 8/3—12/4/24.**G.**
Don. 10/3—5/6/26.**G.**
Don. 18/6—3/8/28.**G.**
Cow. ?/?—?/9/30.**G.**
Don. 17/9—8/10/32.**G.**
Trip cock gear and condensing
gear fitted.
Don. 5—12/11/32.**L.**
Trip cock gear and condensing
gear removed.
Cow. ?/?—7/11/33.**L.**
Cow. ?/?—23/11/34.**G.**
Cow. ?/?—20/6/36.**G.**
Cow. 5/2—1/3/38.**G.**
Cow. ?/?—22/6/40.**G.**
Cow. ?/?—30/11/40.**L.**
Cow. 26/9—31/10/42.**G.**
Cow. 25/8—21/9/45.**G.**
Cow. 22/12/47—12/2/48.**G.**
Cow. 19/1—12/2/49.**H/I.**
Cow. 3/7—7/8/52.**H/I.**
Cow. 22—28/8/52.**N/C.**
Cow. 12/9/52.**N/C.**
Cow. 5/10—6/11/54.**G.**

BOILERS:
7560.
7582 8/10/32.
1382 (ex892) 1/3/38.
C1708 (ex4728) 31/10/42.
9133 (exD1 3051) 12/2/48.
9133 reno.21549 7/8/52.
21542 (ex69596) 6/11/54.

SHEDS:
King's Cross.
St Margarets 17/8/28.
Hatfield 24/9/30.
Kipps 17/11/32.
Parkhead 25/9/51.
Dawsholm 12/5/52.
Parkhead 22/8/57.

RENUMBERED:
4730 12/4/24.
9509 24/3/46.
69509 12/2/49.

CONDEMNED:22/10/60.
C/u at Heatheryknowe 20/1/62.

4731

N.B. Loco. 22587.

To traffic 1/1921.

REPAIRS:
Don. 13—25/3/22.**L.**
Don. 7—26/1/24.**G.**
Don. 9/11/25—16/1/26.**G.**
Don. 4/8—25/10/27.**G.**
Cow. ?/?—?/6/28.**N/C.**
Westinghouse brake fitted.
(Cowlairs records missing).
Cow. 13/11—5/12/31.**G.**
Don. 12/3—16/4/32.**H.**
Cow. ?/?—10/6/33.**G.**
Cow. ?/?—2/11/35.**G.**
Cow. ?/?—19/9/36.**L.**
Cow. 4—21/9/37.**G.**
Cow. ?/?—28/10/39.**G.**
Cow. ?/?—17/2/40.**L.**
Cow. ?/?—22/6/40.**L.**
Cow. ?/?—5/10/40.**L.**
Cow. ?/?—22/4/42.**L.**
Cow. 8—29/5/43.**G.**
Cow. ?/?—11/11/44.**G.**
Cow. 15/2—4/4/47.**G.**
Westinghouse brake removed.
Cow. 27—30/12/48.**G.**
Cow. 12/4—10/6/49.**H/I.**
Cow. ?/?—17/11/49.**C/L.**
Cow. 4—30/8/52.**G.**
Cow. 23—24/6/54.**N/C.**
Cow. 14—30/4/55.**H/I.**
Cow. 27—31/3/56.**N/C.**
Cow. 26/3—19/4/58.**G.**

BOILERS:
7561.
7585 16/4/32.
1365 (ex895) 21/9/37.
1383 (ex2690) 29/5/43.
C1666 (ex4724) 4/4/47.
21537 (ex69503) 30/8/52.
21547 (ex69500) 19/4/58.

SHEDS:
King's Cross.
Scotland 27/10/27.
St Margarets 26/11/27.
Stratford 4/1/32.
Kipps 2/11/32.
Parkhead ?/7/40.
Stratford 17/1/41.
Parkhead 1/10/41.
Kipps 1/10/51.
Parkhead 14/4/52.
Hawick 11/2/57.

RENUMBERED:
4731 26/1/24.
9510 24/3/46.
69510 8/1/49.

(col 4)

CONDEMNED: 4/11/59.
Cut up at Cowlairs 13/2/60.

4732

N.B. Loco. 22588.

To traffic 1/1921.

REPAIRS:
Don. 6—23/2/24.**G.**
Don. 2/12/25—13/3/26.**G.**
Don. 19/1—29/3/28.**G.**
Westinghouse brake fitted.
(Records missing).
???. ?/?—24/2/32.**?.**
Str. ?/9—22/9/32.**G.**
Cow. ?/?—?/11/33.**L.**
Cow. ?/?—?/7/34.**L.**
Cow. ?/?—31/10/34.**G.**
Cow. ?/?—?/11/34.**L.**
Cow. ?/?—19/6/36.**G.**
Cow. ?/?—16/7/36.**L.**
Cow. 16/7—29/8/38.**G.**
Cow. ?/?—5/9/42.**G.**
Cow. ?/?—28/11/42.**L.**
Cow. 16/10—1/11/45.**G.**
Westinghouse brake removed.
Cow. 25—31/10/47.**L.**
Cow. 24/11—27/12/47.**G.**
Cow. 17—26/6/48.**L.**
Cow. ?/?—1/7/49.**N/C.**
Cow. 21/2—8/4/50.**G.**
Cow. 3—18/7/52.**H/I.**
Cow. 24/1—19/2/55.**G.**
Cow. 19—21/4/55.**N/C.**

BOILERS:
7562.
7562 reno. C1674 ?/?/?.
7582 (ex4730) 29/8/38.
C1663 (ex4739) 1/11/45.
8134 (ex9518) 8/4/50.
8134 reno.21544 18/7/52.
21549 (ex69509) 19/2/55.

SHEDS:
King's Cross.
Scotland 11/4/28.
Kipps by 16/5/28.
Stratford 27/2/32.
Kipps 2/11/32.
Stratford 17/1/41.
Kipps 1/10/41.
Parkhead 23/9/51.
Dawsholm 12/5/52.

RENUMBERED:
4732 23/2/24.
9511 12/4/46.
69511 26/6/48.

CONDEMNED: 15/12/60.
Cut up at Cowlairs 4/3/61.

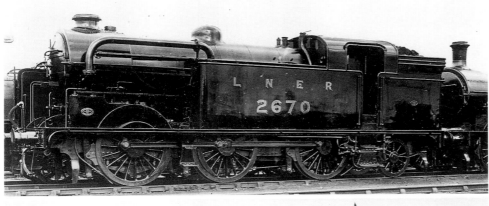

This did not effect a cure, nor did extra baffle plates put inside the tank and in May 1929 No.2680 had its pipes shortened to enter the tank as far forward as possible. During 1930-31 the other nineteen were altered similarly.

The first three, Nos.2682 to 2684, from Yorkshire Engine Co., originally had the GER arrangement of piping for condensing apparatus.

Between 3rd May and 11th September 1930 these three had the condenser pipes shortened to enter the tank close to the front end. Doncaster works, 21st March 1937.

Nos.2685 to 2690 were not fitted for condensing and also had the 4in. taller chimney.

The arrival of the V1 Class in Scotland sent Nos.2685 to 2687 to the London District between 25th November 1930 and 24th October 1931. Doncaster duly added condensing and trip cock gear and changed the chimney to $12\frac{3}{8}$, in. type. Note that destination board brackets were added to the smokebox door although the Scottish type were also retained. The first to arrive in the London District was 2686 which went to Hatfield on 25th November 1930, however, it was not fitted with condensing gear and a short chimney until it visited Doncaster works in December 1931. No.2685 went to Doncaster shed on the 8th July 1931 then into works on 28th August for condensing gear and short chimney then, after coming out on 15th October it went to King's Cross shed. No.2687 was transferred to King's Cross 24th October 1931 but entered works that day for the fitting of the short chimney and condensing gear. On 19th January 1931, No.2688 also moved south, but to Ardsley so did not need alteration or additions. Doncaster shed.

On Nos.2662 to 2690, both cylinder and axlebox lubrication was by Wakefield mechanical No.7 type mounted on the right hand side.

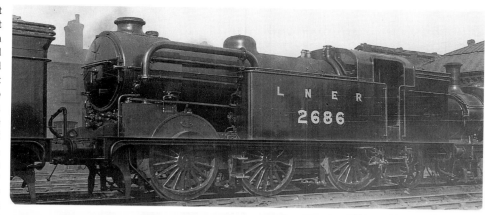

All previous batches had steam applied sanding to the leading wheels but on Nos.2662 to 2690 it was by gravity. The sandboxes were smaller and the lids more watertight.

Squat domes and covers were standard, and not only for engines built to Metropolitan gauge. Ex-Cowlairs 10th March 1933, No.4739 had been fitted with the boiler from D1 class No.3060 and the taller dome needed a higher cover with an almost flat top. The boiler was taken off in May 1939 and was then carried by No.4729 from 30th December 1939 to 26th July 1941 when the boiler was condemned.

4733

N.B. Loco. 22589.

To traffic 1/1921.

REPAIRS:
Don. 7—23/2/24.**G.**
Don. 8/2—18/5/26.**G.**
Don. 18/6—27/7/28.**G.**
Cow. 23—31/8/28.**L.**
Cow. 13/2—16/3/31.**G.**
Cow. 24/3—24/4/31.**N/C.**
Don. 18/7—8/8/31.**L.**
Condensing gear refitted.
Don. 4/3—6/6/33.**G.**
Gor. 24/10—22/12/34.**G.**
Str. 18/8—30/9/36.**G.**
Don. 19/2—5/4/39.**G.**
Don. 16/8—14/9/41.**G.**
Don. 21/2—6/4/44.**G.**
Don. 23/5—20/7/47.**G.**
Don. 6/2—30/3/50.**G.**
Don. 19/6—25/7/52.**G.**
Str. 10/1—5/3/55.**G.**
Str. 14—22/4/55.**N/C.**
Str. 2/2—11/4/58.**G.**

BOILERS:
7563.
7592 27/7/28.
8283 22/12/34.
7678 30/9/36.
9142 5/4/39.
9777 20/7/47.
10558 30/3/50.
21369 25/7/52.
21412 5/3/55.
21370 11/4/58.

SHEDS:
King's Cross.
Scotland 27/7/28.
Dunfermline 12/9/28.
King's Cross 25/4/31.
Hornsey 25/9/60.
New England 9/7/61.

RENUMBERED:
4733 23/2/24.
9512 31/3/46.
69512 30/3/50.

CONDEMNED: 24/7/62.
Into Don. for cut up 24/7/62.

4734

N.B. Loco. 22590.

To traffic 1/1921.

REPAIRS:
Don. 18/1—16/2/24.**G.**
Don. 22/2—22/5/26.**G.**
Don. 14/6—3/8/28.**G.**
Cow. 21/8—4/9/28.**L.**
Cow. 29—31/10/28.**N/C.**
Cow. 1—10/8/29.**L.**
Cow. 14—28/8/29.**N/C.**
Cow. 9/10—13/11/30.**G.**
Cow. 7/2/31.**L.**
Don. 4/4—24/5/32.**G.**
Condensing and trip cock gear
fitted.
Don. 21/10—18/12/33.**G.**
Don. 25/5—11/7/35.**G.**
Str. 13/12/36—26/1/37.**G.**
Str. 21/6—10/8/38.**G.**
T.A.B. valves fitted.
Don. 20/11/39—22/1/40.**G.**
Don. 6/2—11/4/40.**L.**
Str. 20/1—8/6/43.**G.**
Don. 22/5—26/7/46.**G.**
Don. 24/1—28/2/49.**G.**
Don. 8—31/8/51.**G.**
Don. 26/9—12/10/51.**N/C.**
Str. 30/3—22/5/54.**G.**
Str. 22/11/54—15/1/55.**C/L.**
Str. 7/6—29/8/56.**C/L.**
Don. 3/7—16/8/57.**G.**
Don. 18—21/8/57.**N/C.**
Don. 9—27/1/59.**C/L.**

BOILERS:
7564.
7551 24/5/32.
7539 26/1/37.
8996 8/6/43.
8104 26/7/46.
9330 28/2/49.
21301 31/8/51.
21315 22/5/54.
21410 16/8/57.

SHEDS:
King's Cross.
Scotland 15/8/28.
Haymarket 24/8/28.
Southern Area 14/11/30.
Hatfield 18/2/31.
Hornsey 11/12/38.
New England 14/6/59.

RENUMBERED:
4734 16/2/24.
9513 7/4/46.
69513 26/2/49.

CONDEMNED: 29/5/61.
Into Don. for cut up 29/5/61.

4735

N.B. Loco. 22591.

To traffic 1/1921.

REPAIRS:
Don. 13—18/3/22.**L.**
Don. 15/2—22/3/24.**G.**
Don. 26/4—14/8/26.**G.**
Don. 31/1—14/4/28.**G.**
Westinghouse brake fitted.
(Cowlairs records missing).
Cow. 13—31/10/34.**G.**
Cow. ?/?—5/3/36.**G.**
Cow. ?/?—1/4/38.**G.**
Cow. ?/?—14/4/38.**L.**
Cow. ?/?—3/6/39.**L.**
Cow. 30/12/39—17/2/40.**G.**
Cow. 16—30/1/43.**G.**
Cow. ?/?—4/2/43.**L.**
Cow. ?/?—29/5/43.**L.**
Cow. ?/?—?/7/43.**L.**
Cow. ?/?—24/10/45.**L.**
Cow. 30/8—27/9/46.**G.**
Westinghouse brake removed.
Cow. 11/4—14/5/49.**L/I.**
Cow. ?/?—?/10/49.**C/L.**
Cow. 4—30/6/51.**G.**
Cow. 4—7/12/51.**C/L.**
Cow. 3—19/1/52.**N/C.**
Cow. 19—23/5/52.**N/C.**
Inv. 29/3—23/4/54.**L/I.**
Inv. 27/4—7/5/54.**N/C.**
Cow. 2—6/8/55.**N/C.**
Cow. 11/8/55. Not repaired.

BOILERS:
7565.
7565 reno. C1677 ?/?/28.
C1666 (ex4724) 31/10/34.
C1671 (ex4729) 17/2/40.
1382 (ex4730) 30/1/43.
7542 (ex9508) 27/9/46.
21543 (ex69511) 30/6/51.

SHEDS:
King's Cross.
Scotland 26/4/28.
Parkhead 30/5/28.

RENUMBERED:
4735 22/3/24.
9514 24/3/46.
69514 14/5/49.

CONDEMNED: 22/9/55.
Cut up at Cowlairs.

4736

N.B. Loco. 22592.

To traffic 1/1921.

REPAIRS:
Don. 28/8—9/9/22.**L.**
Don. 8/3—12/4/24.**G.**
Don. 3/5—1/9/26.**G.**
Don. 16/6—4/8/28.**G.**
Cow. 16—23/8/28.**L.**
Cow. 7—18/9/28.**N/C.**
Cow. 21/9—6/10/28.**N/C.**
Cow. 25/7—3/8/29.**N/C.**
Cow. 13/8—4/9/29.**N/C.**
Cow. 19—28/9/29.**N/C.**
Cow. 23/10—8/11/29.**N/C.**
Cow. 2/10—3/11/30.**G.**
Cow. 10/11/30—31/1/31.**L.**
Mishap damage.
Don. 27/2—12/5/33.**G.**
Don. 26/11—20/12/35.**G.**
Don. 13/12/37—8/1/38.**G.**
Don. 29/1—5/3/40.**G.**
Don. 17/3—12/4/40.**L.**
Str. 29/11/42—14/3/43.**G.**
Don. 10/9—9/10/45.**G.**
Don. 25/7—29/8/48.**G.**
Don. 14/11—7/12/51.**G.**
Str. 20/2—26/3/55.**G.**

BOILERS:
7566.
7560 12/5/33.
9065 8/1/38.
9066 29/8/48.
21327 7/12/51.
21416 26/3/55.

SHEDS:
King's Cross.
Scotland 14/8/28.
Kipps 24/8/28.
Ardsley 6/2/31.
Bradford 26/3/41.
Doncaster 3/11/41.
King's Cross 29/11/41.
Hatfield 7/12/41.
King's Cross 5/3/44.
Hitchin 28/4/46.

RENUMBERED:
4736 12/4/24.
9515 24/3/46.
69515 28/8/48.

CONDEMNED: 22/7/59.
Into Don. for cut up 22/7/59

4737

N.B. Loco. 22593.

To traffic 2/1921.

REPAIRS:
Don. 20/2—29/3/24.**G.**
Don. 23/10—19/12/25.**G.**
Don. 5/8—27/10/27.**G.**
Cow. 29/12/27—16/1/28.**L.**
Cow. 2—28/2/28.**L.**
Dual brake fitted.
Cow. 28/8—10/10/28.**G.**
Cow. 20/10—13/11/28.**N/C.**

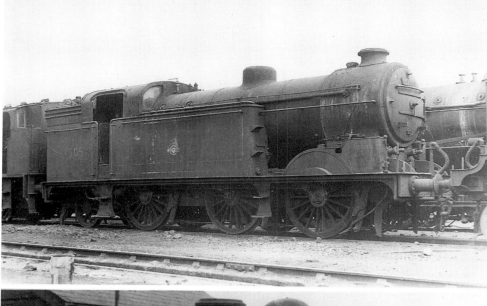

Ex-works 8th February 1947, No.9505 had been fitted with a 1929 built boiler hitherto used on J6 and D2 classes. The taller dome needed a higher cover which was then retained to withdrawal although the 1929 boiler was taken off from 14th February 1950 to be cut up. Grantham, March 1960.

The only other departure from the squat dome cover was on No.69559 which was ex-Doncaster works 28th October 1952 with a boiler built in December 1937 for J6 class No.3629 and which had been on N2 No.9574 from 7th December 1946 to 29th May 1952. That had been built with a low dome so No.9574 used a normal cover and No.69559 got an N1 type cover only as an expediency, but then kept it to 18th July 1957 withdrawal. Wood Green, circa 1953.

The seventy-eight engines to No.897 built in December 1925 were fitted originally with Ramsbottom safety valves. All subsequent boilers had Ross 'pop' type.

Replacement boilers for the first seventy-eight engines had Ross 'pop' safety valves.

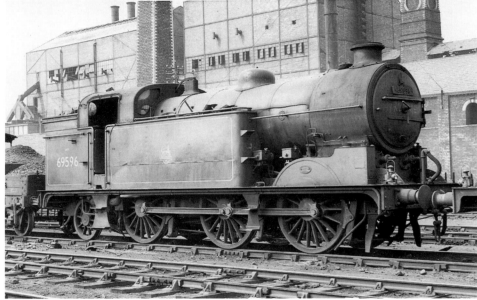

(left) The softer water in Scotland gave boilers a much longer life and nine N2's working there: 69503, 69507, 69508, 69509, 69514, 69553, 69563, 69565 and 69596 still had boilers with Ramsbottom valves when withdrawn between 1957 and 1960. No.69596's boiler started work in January 1921 on No.1728 and was withdrawn on 2nd September 1960 along with that engine. Note that the vacuum ejector exhaust through the boiler was made external on left hand drive engines.

(below) In accordance with their later practice, Cowlairs fitted a rectangular cover at the base of Ross 'pop' valves. Eastfield shed.

4737 cont./

Don. 21/2—15/5/31.**G.**
Str. 19/4—5/9/34.**G.**
Str. 22/12/36—2/2/37.**G.**
Str. 26/1—15/3/40.**G.**
Westinghouse brake removed.
Str. 16/6—10/9/42.**G.**
Don. 14/8—13/9/44.**G.**
Don. 25/2—21/4/47.**G.**
Don. 12/12/49—13/1/50.**G.**
Don. 10/4—6/5/53.**G.**
Don. 12/12/56—24/1/57.**G.**
Don. 28—30/1/57.**N/C.**

BOILERS:
7567.
7574 15/5/31.
7542 2/2/37.
9063 15/3/40.
8540 13/9/44.
10554 13/1/50.
21460 6/5/53.
21278 24/1/57.

SHEDS:
King's Cross.
Eastfield 4 to 8/24 *(on loan).*
Scotland 23/12/27.
Eastfield 31/12/27.
Haymarket 28/2/28.
Southern Area 7/5/29.*
Stratford 9/5/29.
Hatfield 26/3/40.
Neasden 11/2/45.
Hornsey 11/11/47.
King's Cross 9/9/51.
Hatfield 18/5/52.
King's Cross 31/5/53.
Hatfield 15/11/53.
King's Cross 20/6/54.
Hatfield 22/8/54.
King's Cross 16/3/58.
Hornsey 18/5/58.
Grantham 16/11/58.
*On loan to GE Section 6/5/29,
permanent from 31/10/30.*

RENUMBERED:
4737 29/3/24.
9516 24/3/46.
69516 13/1/50.

CONDEMNED: 23/1/61.
Into Don. for cut up 26/1/61.

4738

N.B. Loco. 22594.

To traffic 2/1921.

REPAIRS:
Don. 20/2—29/3/24.**G.**
Don. 5/7—26/10/26.**G.**
Don. 22/6—10/8/28.**G.**
Cow. 28—29/8/28.**N/C.**
Don. 1/4—9/5/31.**G.**
Don. 30/5—23/7/31.**N/C.**
*Condensing and trip cock gear
fitted.*
Don. 17/12/32—21/2/33**G.**
Gor. 5/10—1/12/34.**G.**
Str. 23/8—14/10/36.**G.**
Str. 22/10/38—3/1/39.**G.**
Don. 12/4—17/5/41.**G.**
Don. 30/8—25/9/44.**G.**
Don. 5/8—19/9/47.**G.**
Don. 23/5—23/6/50.**G.**
Don. 13/10—2/11/50.**C/L.**
Don. 19/5—18/6/53.**G.**
Str. 23/5—3/7/54.**C/L.**
Str. 5/3—26/4/56.**G.**
Don. 16—30/5/58.**C/L.**

BOILERS:
7568.
7557 21/2/33.
7543 3/1/39.
9266 17/5/41.
9783 19/9/47.
8547 23/6/50.
21464 18/6/53.
21461 26/4/56.

SHEDS:
King's Cross.
Scotland 22/8/28.
Dunfermline 31/8/28.
Eastfield 29/4/30.
St Margarets 3/12/30.
King's Cross 12/5/31.
Colwick 19/1/47.
King's Cross 10/11/47.

RENUMBERED:
4738 29/3/24.
9517 26/5/46.
69517 23/6/50.

CONDEMNED: 8/8/59.
Into Don. for cut up 8/8/59.

4739

N.B. Loco. 22595.

To traffic 2/1921.

REPAIRS:
Don. 16/5—2/6/23.**L.**
Don. 12/3—26/4/24.**G.**

Don. 21/6—9/10/26.**G.**
Don. 26/6—10/8/28.**G.**
(Cowlairs records missing).
Cow. ?/?—10/3/33.**G.**
(Cowlairs records missing).
Cow. ?/?—13/3/37.**G.**
Cow. ?/?—4/3/37.**N/C.**
*Destination board brackets
fitted on smokebox.*
Cow. ?/?—17/6/39.**G.**
Cow. ?/?—29/6/40.**L.**
Cow. ?/?—9/11/40.**L.**
Cow. ?/?—14/3/42.**G.**
Cow. 16/12/44—13/1/45.**G.**
Cow. 19/4—10/5/47.**G.**
Cow. 20/12/49—20/1/50.**G.**
Cow. 19—20/6/51.**N/C.**
Cow. 8/2—5/3/55.**G.**

BOILERS:
7569.
7569 reno.C1681 ?/?/?.
7417 *(exD1 3060)* 10/3/33.
C1663 *(ex4721)* 17/6/39.
8134 *(ex4731)* 13/1/45.
7585 *(ex9565)* 20/1/50.
21544 *(ex69511)* 5/3/55.

SHEDS:
King's Cross.
Scotland 21/8/28.
Haymarket 31/8/28.
St Margarets ?/10/28.
Duns 1/4/29.
Heaton 12/7/34.
St Margarets 6/7/36.
Kipps 5/10/40.

RENUMBERED:
4739 26/4/24.
9518 12/5/46.
69518 20/1/50.

CONDEMNED: 16/1/61.
C/u at Heatheryknowe 20/5/61.

4740

N.B. Loco. 22596.

To traffic 2/1921.

REPAIRS:
Don. 10—20/1/23.**L.**
Don. 13/3—19/4/24.**G.**
Don. 2/2—17/4/26.**G.**
Don. 9/6—28/7/28.**G.**
Cow. 9—28/8/28.**N/C.**
Dual brake fitted.
Cow. 20/5—3/7/30.**G.**

Cow. 29/2—20/4/32.**G.**
Cow. 22—25/4/32.**N/C.**
Str. 11/6—7/10/32.**H.**
Str. 10/2—10/4/35.**G.**
Str. 7/2—31/3/37.**G.**
Str. 30/1—9/2/40.**L.**
Westinghouse brake removed.
Don. 3/4—16/5/40.**G.**
Don. 15/2—17/4/42.**G.**
Don. 29/10—8/12/45.**G.**
Don. 3/5—4/6/48.**G.**
Don. 14/2—9/3/51.**G.**
Str. 28/11/55—21/1/56.**G.**

BOILERS:
7570.
7570 reno.C1682 3/7/30.
7580 31/3/37.
9222 16/5/40.
8941 8/12/45.
21251 9/3/51.
21222 21/1/56.

SHEDS:
King's Cross.
Ardsley 25/4/26.
King's Cross 1/1/27.
Scotland 28/7/28.
Dundee 8/8/28.
Stratford 9/5/32.
Hatfield 13/2/40.
Doncaster 2/5/42.
Mexborough 9/5/42.
Neasden 2/2/44.
King's Cross 6/6/48.

RENUMBERED:
4740 19/4/24.
9519 28/4/46.
69519 4/6/48.

CONDEMNED: 11/10/57.
Into Don. for cut up 11/10/57.

4741

N.B. Loco. 22597.

To traffic 2/1921.

REPAIRS:
Don. 13—25/3/32.**L.**
Don. 6/2—8/3/24.**G.**
Don. 9/6—12/7/24.**L.**
Don. 3/8—5/11/26.**G.**
Don. 13/12/28—14/2/29.**G.**
Don. 3/10—27/11/30.**G.**
Don. 2/7—1/10/32.**G.**
Gor. 31/3—2/6/34.**G.**
Don. 24/3—25/4/36.**G.**

WORKS CODES:- Bpk - Beyer, Peacock. Cow - Cowlairs. Dar- Darlington. Don - Doncaster. Ghd - Gateshead. Gor - Gorton. Inv - Inverurie. Str - Stratford.
REPAIR CODES:- **C/H** - Casual Heavy. **C/L** - Casual Light. **G** - General. **H**- Heavy. **H/I** - Heavy Intermediate. **L** - Light. **L/I** - Light Intermediate. **N/C** - Non-Classified.

61

New boilers, and new firebox casings fitted 1936 onwards had inspection covers instead of washout plugs.

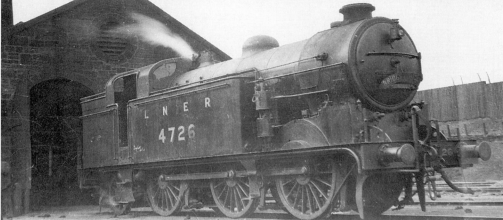

The first sixty engines had right hand drive and the vacuum ejector exhaust pipe passed through the boiler barrel.

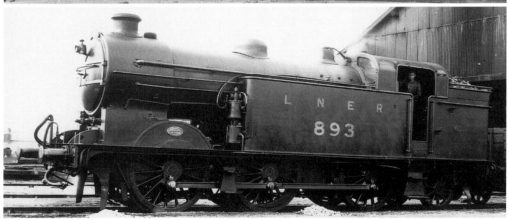

On post-Grouping engines the ejector exhaust pipe was external on the left hand side and pitched 9in. above the boiler centre line.

From 1931 all exhaust pipes were put outside the boiler barrel and on the first sixty boilers were on the right hand side. Eastfield shed.

When new the first sixty had a combination injector in the cab and a hot water under-footplate injector on the left hand side. Eastfield shed.

As they were condensing engines, a Westinghouse steam driven feed pump was provided on the right hand side.

The Part 2 and 3 engines built in 1925 did not have condensing apparatus, so simply had two combination injectors mounted on the faceplate in the cab.

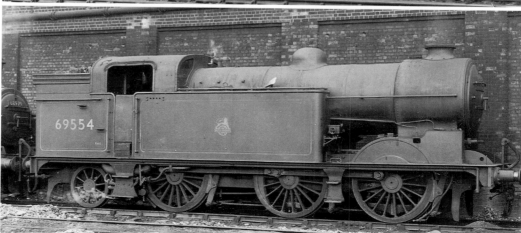

Some of these 1925 builds were changed at a later date to under-footplate injector. No.2587 became 9554 from 28th July 1946. It moved from Scotland to the West Riding on 27th July 1931 and then on 29th November 1941 to the London district for which Doncaster changed its $16^{3}/_{8}$, in. chimney to $12^{3}/_{8}$, in., ex-works 8th November 1941.

4741 cont./

Str. 3/5—22/6/38.**G.**
T.A.B. valves fitted.
Don. 8/6—11/8/39.**G.**
Don. 24/4—3/7/40.**L.**
Str. 24/4—26/11/43.**G.**
Don. 11/7—25/8/45.**L.**
Str. 14/11/46—10/3/47.**G.**
Don. 8/2—10/3/49.**G.**
Don. 9/9—11/10/51.**G.**
Don. 8—23/11/51.**N/C.**
Don. 5/2—30/4/53.**C/H.**
Str. 29/4—11/6/55.**G.**
Don. 3/11—12/12/58.**G.**

BOILERS:
7571.
7580 27/11/30.
7568 2/6/34.
9178 11/8/39.
9179 10/3/49.
21310 11/10/51.
21327 11/6/55.
21470 12/12/58.

SHEDS:
King's Cross.
Hornsey 15/11/59.
New England 9/7/61.

RENUMBERED:
4741 8/3/24.
9520 12/5/46.
69520 10/3/49.

CONDEMNED: 23/9/62.
Into Don. for cut up 20/2/63.

4742

N.B. Loco. 22598.

To traffic 2/1921.

REPAIRS:
Don. 4—15/4/22.**L.**
Don. 20/2—8/3/24.**G.**
Don. 17/3—6/7/28.**G.**
Don. 28/12/29—8/2/30.**G.**
Don. 22/8—15/10/31.**G.**
Don. 12/5—4/8/33.**G.**
Don. 10/12/34—19/1/35.**G.**
Str. 8/11—22/12/36.**G.**
Don. 24/2—20/4/39.**G.**
Don. 11/12/41—30/1/42.**G.**
Don. 9/12/44—24/1/45.**G.**
Don. 20/10—25/11/47.**G.**
Don. 18—27/2/48.**L.**
Don. 12/10—23/11/48.**L.**
Don. 21/6—24/7/50.**G.**
Don. 31/12/53—30/1/54.**G.**
Str. 3/2—29/3/56.**C/H.**
Don. 4—28/2/57.**G.**
Don. 7—9/3/57.**N/C.**

BOILERS:
7572.
7552 6/7/28.
7542 4/8/33.
7592 22/12/36.
9145 20/4/39.
8995 25/11/47.
9783 24/7/50.
21258 30/1/54.
21206 29/3/56.
21460 28/2/57.

SHEDS:
King's Cross.
New England 26/7/59.

RENUMBERED:
4742 8/3/24.
9521 18/5/46.
69521 23/11/48.

CONDEMNED: 1/6/61.
Into Don. for cut up 1/6/61.

4743

N.B. Loco. 22599.

To traffic 2/1921.

REPAIRS:
Don. 1—17/3/23.**L.**
Don. 8/3—5/4/24.**G.**
Don. 7/11/25—9/1/26.**G.**
Don. 19/11/27—28/1/28.**G.**
Don. 12/10—11/12/29.**G.**
Don. 4/7—28/8/31.**G.**
Don. 4/2—13/4/33.**G.**
Don. 11/1—6/2/35.**G.**
Don. 23/8—9/10/36.**G.**
Str. 9/9—2/12/38.**G.**
Don. 17/5—21/6/41.**G.**
Don. 8—29/7/44.**G.**
Don. 12/9—9/11/46.**G.**
Repainted green.
Don. 15/5—10/6/49.**G.**
Painted black again.
Don. 19/11/50—2/1/51.**H/I.**
Don. 16/4—11/5/53.**G.**
Str. 29/5—28/7/56.**G.**
Str. 15—21/8/56.**N/C.**

BOILERS:
7573.
7551 28/1/28.
7680 11/12/29.
7541 9/10/36.
7573 2/12/38.
8282 21/6/41.
8940 29/7/44.
8938 10/6/49.
8938 reno.21231 2/1/51.
21239 11/5/53.
21377 28/7/56.

SHEDS:
King's Cross.
Neasden 11/2/45.
Hornsey 11/9/47.
King's Cross 9/9/51.
Hornsey 19/10/52.
Hitchin 12/7/59.

RENUMBERED:
4743 5/4/24.
9522 28/4/46.
69522 10/6/49.

CONDEMNED: 23/11/59.
Into Don. for cut up 23/11/59.

4744

N.B. Loco. 22600.

To traffic 2/1921.

REPAIRS:
Don. 28/8—2/9/22.**L.**
Don. 15/2—22/3/24.**G.**
Don. 20/2—22/6/26.**G.**
Don. 14/8—10/10/28.**G.**
Don. 25/1—11/3/30.**G.**
Don. 22/10—28/12/31.**G.**
Don. 9/11/33—5/1/34.**G.**
Don. 23/10—23/11/35.**G.**
Don. 14/9—12/10/37.**G.**
Str. 26/8—27/10/39.**G.**
Str. 23/2—15/5/43.**G.**
Don. 17/1—22/2/44.**H.**
Don. 10/3—6/4/46.**G.**
Don. 6/12/48—12/1/49.**G.**
Don. 24—28/1/49.**N/C.**
Don. 10/1—17/3/50.**G.**
Don. 11—29/9/50.**C/L.**
Don. 6/12/51—10/1/52.**C/H.**
Don. 16/1—11/2/53.**G.**
Str. 16/5—30/6/55.**G.**
Don. 17/5—8/7/58.**G.**
Don. 13/2/63. *Not repaired.*

BOILERS:
7574.
7577 11/3/30.
9063 12/10/37.
8996 27/10/39.
9176 15/5/43.
9335 6/4/46.
9335 reno.21209 29/9/50.
21451 11/2/53.
21398 30/6/55.
21529 8/7/58.

SHEDS:
King's Cross.
New England 20/5/62.

RENUMBERED:
4744 22/3/24.
9523 10/12/46.
69523 12/1/49.

WITHDRAWN: 16/9/62.
*Purchased for preservation by
the Gresley Society.*

4745

N.B. Loco. 22601.

To traffic 2/1921.

REPAIRS:
Don. 24/2—11/3/22.**L.**
Don. 20—30/6/23.**L.**
Don. 7/1—9/2/24.**G.**
Don. 25/1—23/3/26.**G.**
Don. 17/9—25/10/26.**L.**
Don. 15/6—17/8/28.**G.**
Don. 11/1—25/2/30.**G.**
Don. 10/10—7/12/31.**G.**
Don. 9/9—26/10/33.**G.**
Don. 3/5—15/6/35.**G.**
Don. 7/3—27/4/37.**G.**
Str. 18/3—17/5/39.**G.**
Don. 14/6—21/7/41.**G.**
Don. 15/7—19/8/44.**G.**
Don. 28/1—16/3/46.**G.**
Don. 6/7—29/8/48.**G.**
Don. 12/2—7/3/51.**G.**
Don. 21/11—18/12/51.**C/L.**
Don. 16/9—15/10/53.**G.**
Str. 5/3—2/4/54.**C/L.**
Str. 11/11/54—15/1/55.**C/L.**
Don. 16/11/56—2/1/57.**G.**
Don. 4—5/1/57.**N/C.**
Don. 3—14/2/58.**N/C.**
Don. 13/6—9/7/58.**C/L.**

BOILERS:
7575.
7551 25/2/30.
7579 7/12/31.
7680 17/5/39.
9610 16/3/46.
21244 7/3/51.
21243 15/10/53.
21272 2/1/57.

SHED:
King's Cross.

RENUMBERED:
4745 9/2/24.
9524 9/1/47.
69524 28/8/48.

CONDEMNED: 2/11/59.
Into Don. for cut up 2/11/59.

From 1926 it became standard for the first sixty engines to change to under-footplate injector on the right hand side. Eastfield shed.

(above) With this injector change the Westinghouse feed pump was then taken off. No.4747 ex-works 19th December 1925 was the first to lose the pump.

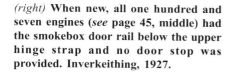

(right) When new, all one hundred and seven engines (see page 45, middle) had the smokebox door rail below the upper hinge strap and no door stop was provided. Inverkeithing, 1927.

From about 1930 engines in Southern Area had the rail moved above the strap and a door stop was fitted between the hinges. Note the strengthening plate for attaching the coupling hook. Not all were so fitted as the illustration at the bottom of page 86 shows.

Of the engines maintained by Cowlairs only 69508, 69511, 69518 and 69553 had the rail position altered (*see* page 82, top) and the others kept to the original position. Parkhead shed, April 1958.

(below) Another rail oddity was No.69523 which was fitted with a short rail above the number plate, and which it then kept to withdrawal. Indeed, as restored to No. 4744 it still has this odd rail. Doncaster works, July 1963.

(above) From January 1950 to September 1954, Parkhead shedded No.69564 had a curved rail of the type Cowlairs reserved for superheated engines. It then reverted to normal type as in the view on page 72, top shows. Parkhead, September 1953.

4746

N.B. Loco. 22602.

To traffic 2/1921.

REPAIRS:
Don. 24/2—4/3/22.**L.**
Don. 26/3—10/5/24.**G.**
Handrail fitted on bunker.
Don. 27/8—22/12/26.**G.**
Don. 29/12/28—1/3/29.**G.**
Don. 22/5—12/8/31.**G.**
Don. 26/8—19/10/33.**G.**
Don. 24/5—29/6/35.**G.**
Don. 24/2—12/4/37.**G.**
Str. 11/3—28/4/39.**G.**
Don. 5/10—12/11/41.**G.**
Don. 19/8—16/9/44.**G.**
Don. 28/5—18/7/47.**G.**
Don. 19/3—23/4/48.**H.**
Don. 12/7—4/8/50.**G.**
Don. 10—13/10/50.**C/L.**
Don. 15/3—16/4/53.**G.**
Str. 20/7—10/9/55.**G.**

BOILERS:
7576.
7584 12/8/31.
7595 28/4/39.
8135 12/11/41.
9137 4/8/50.
21456 16/4/53.
21367 10/9/55.

SHEDS:
King's Cross.
Hornsey 6/10/57.
King's Cross 27/7/58.

RENUMBERED:
4746 10/5/24.
9525 28/9/46.
69525 23/4/48.

CONDEMNED: 4/3/59.
Into Don. for cut up 4/3/59.

4747

N.B. Loco. 22603.

To traffic 2/1921.

REPAIRS:
Don. 10—27/1/23.**L.**
Don. 19/3—3/5/24.**G.**
Don. 23/10—19/12/25.**G.**
Don. 12/10—9/12/27.**G.**
Don. 6/4/28.**N/C.**
Don. 20/7—23/8/29.**G.**
Don. 27/3—15/6/31.**G.**
Don. 18/3—19/6/33.**G.**
Don. 25/1—2/3/35.**G.**

Str. 30/12/36—20/2/37.**G.**
Str. 15/7—31/8/38.**G.**
Don. 2/5—6/6/41.**G.**
Don. 15/6—20/7/44.**G.**
Don. 1/9—13/10/47.**G.**
Don. 16/1—7/2/51.**G.**
Don. 23/3—28/4/52.**C/H.**
Don. 30/11/53—4/1/54.**G.**
Don. 17/8—28/9/56.**G.**

BOILERS:
7577.
7598 23/8/29.
7551 20/2/37.
7576 31/8/38.
9265 6/6/41.
9266 13/10/47.
21236 7/2/51.
21264 4/1/54.
21464 28/9/56.

SHED:
King's Cross.

RENUMBERED:
4747 3/5/24.
9526 8/12/46.
69526 7/2/51.

CONDEMNED: 10/8/59.
Into Don. for cut up 10/8/59.

4748

N.B. Loco. 22604.

To traffic 2/1921.

REPAIRS:
Don. 18/7—2/8/22.**L.**
Don. 28/2—5/4/24.**G.**
Don. 3/8—11/11/26.**G.**
Don. 14/12/28—16/2/29.**G.**
Don. 27/1—20/3/31.**G.**
Don. 21/1—20/4/33.**G.**
T.A.B. valves fitted.
Don. 9/10—8/12/34.**G.**
Str. 13/9—22/10/36.**G.**
Str. 27/10/38—6/2/39.**G.**
Don. 14/5—12/6/41.**G.**
Don. 28/12/43—27/1/44.**G.**
Don. 21/10—7/12/46.**G.**
Don. 5/9—24/10/49.**G.**
Don. 23/4—22/5/52.**G.**
Str. 20/4—29/5/54.**C/L.**
Str. 18/7—3/9/55.**G.**

BOILERS:
7578.
8283 20/3/31.
7573 8/12/34.
8283 22/10/36.
7541 6/2/39.
9268 12/6/41.

8940 24/10/49.
21358 22/5/52.
21451 3/9/55.

SHED:
King's Cross.

RENUMBERED:
4748 5/4/24.
9527 9/1/47.
69527 24/10/49.

CONDEMNED: 11/6/58.
Into Don. for cut up 11/6/58.

4749

N.B. Loco. 22605.

To traffic 2/1921.

REPAIRS:
Don. 2/12/21—18/1/22.**L.**
Don. 30/1—17/2/23.**L.**
Don. 4/10—28/12/23.**G.**
Don. 5/8—10/10/25.**G.**
Don. 26/7—27/10/27.**G.**
Don. 10/5—18/6/29.**G.**
Don. 25/4—14/7/31.**G.**
Don. 21/4—3/8/33.**G.**
Don. 8/2—8/3/35.**G.**
Don. 8/11/36—8/1/37.**G.**
Str. 20/10/38—20/1/39.**G.**
Don. 8/10—29/11/41.**G.**
Don. 20/7—19/8/44.**G.**
Don. 24/2—13/4/46.**L.**
Don. 7/11—28/12/46.**G.**
Don. 1/12/47—13/1/48.**H.**
Don. 17/7—20/8/49.**G.**
Don. 6—31/3/50.**C/H.**
Don. 8/4—8/5/52.**G.**
Str. 1/9—9/10/54.**G.**
Don. 9/4—30/5/57.**G.**

BOILERS:
7579.
7539 14/7/31.
7543 3/8/33.
7563 8/1/37.
7557 20/1/39.
8136 29/11/41.
9145 13/1/48.
9224 20/8/49.
9145 31/3/50.
21413 *(new)* 8/5/52.
21301 9/10/54.
21207 30/5/57.

SHED:
King's Cross.

RENUMBERED:
1749ₙ 28/12/23.
4749 ?/2/25.

9528 14/12/46.
69528 20/8/49.

CONDEMNED: 25/11/59.
Into Don. for cut up 25/11/59.

4750

N.B. Loco. 22606.

To traffic 2/1921.

REPAIRS:
Don. 2—27/5/22.**L.**
Don. 5—21/10/22.**L.**
Don. 7/1—16/2/24.**G.**
Don. 8/2—22/4/26.**G.**
Don. 22/9—14/11/28.**G.**
Don. 20/3—1/5/30.**G.**
Don. 31/10/31—14/1/32.**G.**
Don. 27/10—15/12/33.**G.**
Don. 6/7—24/8/35.**G.**
Don. 17/3—24/5/37.**G.**
Str. 24/8—25/10/39.**G.**
Don. 14/11—10/12/42.**G.**
Don. 22/8—29/9/45.**G.**
Don. 10/5—18/6/48.**G.**
Don. 4/7—27/8/48.**L.**
Don. 24/3—18/4/51.**G.**
Don. 7/10—6/11/53.**G.**
Don. 17/4—19/5/56.**G.**
Don. 16/3—22/4/59.**G.**

BOILERS:
7580.
7596 1/5/30.
8282 24/5/37.
7679 25/10/39.
9061 29/9/45.
21261 18/4/51.
21244 6/11/53.
21408 22/4/59.

SHEDS:
King's Cross.
Neasden 25/4/26.
King's Cross 27/1/28.
New England 10/9/61.

RENUMBERED:
4750 16/2/24.
9529 28/9/46.
69529 18/6/48.

CONDEMNED: 23/9/62.
Into Don. for cut up 12/3/63.

Ex-Doncaster on 9th February 1928, No.4767 had been fitted with Ashcroft cut-off control, which it retained until it went to works on 27th October 1933, and when ex-works 31st August 1931 - as here - it had been fitted with Trofinoff automatic by-pass valves. Nos.4748 and 4762 got these valves in April and July 1933, and from May to August 1938 ten more were fitted with them:- 2670, 2676, 2678, 2681, 4608, 4734, 4741, 4751, 4752 and 4766.

Ex-works 27th July 1934 from a light repair, No.2686 was fitted with Stone's automatic drifting valve for coasting with the regulator closed. Its removal date was not recorded on the engine's history sheet.

4751

N.B. Loco. 22607.

To traffic 3/1921.

REPAIRS:
Don. 4—15/4/22.**L.**
Don. 5/1—9/2/24.**G.**
Don. 31/7—3/10/25.**G.**
Don. 19/8—9/11/27.**G.**
Don. 12/9—9/11/29.**G.**
Don. 5/11/31—3/2/32.**G.**
Don. 2/2—17/4/34.**G.**
Don. 18/7—24/8/36.**G.**
Str. 20/5—9/7/38.**G.**
T.A.B. valves fitted.
Don. 10/11—5/12/40.**G.**
Str. 29/8—18/10/42.**H.**
Don. 7/4—9/7/43.**G.**
Don. 17/5—21/6/47.**G.**
Don. 21/12/49—27/1/50.**G.**
Don. 8/7—8/8/52.**G.**
Str. 4/10—6/11/54.**G.**
Don. 4/3—9/4/57.**G.**

BOILERS:
7581.
7596 9/11/27.
7600 9/11/29.
8994 24/8/36.
10533 27/1/50.
21370 8/8/52.
21414 6/11/54.
21236 9/4/57.

SHEDS:
Hornsey.
Hitchin 8/6/42.
Hornsey 7/8/46.

RENUMBERED:
4751 9/2/24.
9530 27/7/46.
69530 27/1/50.

CONDEMNED: 29/12/59.
Into Str. for cut up 29/12/59.

4752

N.B. Loco. 22608.

To traffic 3/1921.

REPAIRS:
Don. 28/2—5/4/24.**G.**
Don. 28/9—13/2/26.**G.**
Don. 1/12/28—23/2/29.**G.**
Don. 16/10—15/12/31.**G.**
Don. 14/3—9/6/34.**G.**
Don. 2/5—6/6/36.**G.**
Str. 21/6—28/7/38.**G.**
T.A.B. valves fitted.

Don. 24/2—29/3/41.**G.**
Don. 31/3—6/5/44.**G.**
Don. 19/11/46—18/1/47.**G.**
Don. 9/10—11/11/49.**G.**
Don. 5/6—11/7/52.**G.**
Don. 12/10—10/12/53.**C/L.**
Str. 17/1—19/2/55.**G.**
Str. 17/11/57—10/1/58.**G.**

BOILERS:
7582.
7576 15/12/31.
7536 28/7/38.
7591 29/3/41.
1368 6/5/44.
9223 18/1/47.
8990 11/11/49.
21416 *(new)* 11/7/52.
21419 19/2/55.
21340 10/1/58.

SHEDS:
Hornsey.
Hitchin 1/2/59.
Hatfield 5/4/59.
Grantham 12/6/60.
New England 21/5/61.

RENUMBERED:
4752 5/4/24.
9531 10/8/46.
69531 11/11/49.

CONDEMNED: 7/7/61
Into Don. for cut up 7/7/61.

4753

N.B. Loco. 22609.

To traffic 3/1921.

REPAIRS:
Don. 16/5—2/6/23.**L.**
Don. 17/4—24/5/24.**G.**
Don. 21/6—29/9/26.**G.**
Don. 2/10/28—5/1/29.**G.**
Don. 20/4—22/7/31.**G.**
Don. 22/5—11/8/33.**G.**
Don. 1/8—18/9/35.**G.**
Don. 30/11—15/1/38.**G.**
Don. 5/5—5/6/40.**G.**
Don. 9—30/12/43.**G.**
Don. 18/1—16/3/46.**G.**
Don. 10/9—28/12/46.**H.**
Don. 12/1—7/2/47.**H.**
Don. 7/8—14/9/48.**G.**
Don. 6/3—5/4/51.**G.**
Don. 28/11/51—11/1/52.**C/L.**
Don. 15/8—5/9/52.**C/L.**
Don. 9/12/53—7/1/54.**G.**
Don. 14/6—21/7/56.**G.**

BOILERS:
7583.
7591 5/1/29.
7538 15/1/38.
8094 5/6/40.
1366 30/12/43.
8566 7/2/47.
21258 5/4/51.
21275 7/1/54.
21215 21/7/56.

SHEDS:
Hornsey.
King's Cross 3/6/47.

RENUMBERED:
4753 24/5/24.
9532 16/3/46.
69532 14/9/48.

CONDEMNED: 2/6/59.
Into Don. for cut up 2/6/59.

4754

N.B. Loco. 22610.

To traffic 3/1921.

REPAIRS:
Don. 22/3—7/4/23.**L.**
Don. 15/2—15/3/24.**G.**
Don. 17/8—3/12/26.**G.**
Don. 2/7—5/9/28.**G.**
Don. 8/11/30—12/1/31.**G.**
Don. 19/11/32—31/1/33.**G.**
Don. 31/5—6/7/35.**G.**
Don. 13/4—31/5/37.**G.**
Don. 27/7—3/9/39.**G.**
Don. 24—28/9/39.**N/C.**
Don. 8—28/8/43.**G.**
Don. 27/8—26/10/46.**G.**
Don. 5—29/7/49.**G.**
Don. 16/5—13/6/52.**G.**
Str. 11/3—7/5/54.**C/L.**
Str. 21/12/54—29/1/55.**G.**
Str. 17—25/2/55.**N/C.**
Don. 8/2—8/3/58.**G.**

BOILERS:
7584.
7545 12/1/31.
7544 3/9/39.
9337 26/10/46.
8984 29/7/49.
21415 *(new)* 13/6/52.
21360 29/1/55.
21250 8/3/58.

SHEDS:
Hornsey.
King's Cross 15/11/59.

RENUMBERED:
4754 15/3/24.
9533 10/8/46.
69533 29/7/49.

CONDEMNED: 26/9/61.
Into Don. for cut up 26/9/61.

4755

N.B. Loco. 22611.

To traffic 3/1921.

REPAIRS:
Don. 26/3—3/5/24.**G.**
Don. 20/2—30/4/26.**G.**
Don. 20/8—6/11/28.**G.**
Don. 20/4—18/7/31.**G.**
Don. 29/9—10/11/33.**G.**
Don. 11/10—21/11/35.**G.**
Str. 8/2—6/4/38.**G.**
Don. 3/1—6/2/41.**G.**
Don. 12/1—11/2/44.**G.**
Don. 12/7—31/8/46.**G.**
Don. 30/8—6/10/48.**G.**
Don. 17/8—2/10/50.**G.**
Don. 3—30/11/53.**G.**
Don. 29/9—3/11/56.**G.**
Don. 2/2/59. *Not repaired.*

BOILERS:
7585.
7544 18/7/31.
7566 10/11/33.
7591 6/4/38.
9225 6/2/41.
8996 31/8/46.
9264 6/10/48.
21205 2/10/50.
21312 30/11/53.
21466 3/11/56.

SHEDS:
Hornsey.
Hatfield 8/6/42.
King's Cross 20/12/53.
Hatfield 14/2/54.
Hornsey 18/5/58.

RENUMBERED:
4755 3/5/24.
9534 31/8/46.
69534 2/10/48.

CONDEMNED: 9/2/59.
Cut up at Doncaster.

The seventy-eight engines built to the end of 1925 were fitted with steam sanding at the front but, behind the rear coupled wheels was gravity applied. The latter proved to be more reliable and effective. King's Cross shed.

(above) The final twenty-nine engines, Nos.2662 to 2690 were thus fitted from new at both ends with gravity sanding.

(right) On the engines based in Scotland, all except two had steam sanding at the front changed to gravity applied. Parkhead shed, September 1953.

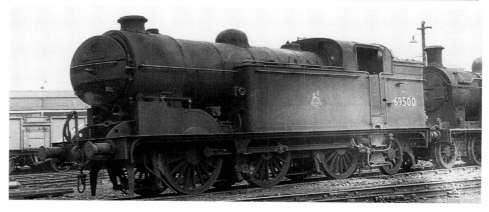

(left) The two Scottish engines to retain steam sanding were Nos.69563 and 69564, which worked mainly from Parkhead. Note the electrification warning flashes on the boiler and cab. No.69564 is at Eastfield shed awaiting transfer to Cowlairs works for scrapping.

(below) Ex-works 14th February, No.4614, and on 21st February 1933, No.4763, were fitted with rail washing gear and their front sanding was changed from steam to gravity applied. Doncaster shed, April 1939.

The rail washing gear was taken off during the 1939-45 war but both - as 9498 and 9542 - kept their gravity sanding. When the BR lettering was discarded in July 1949, the emblem transfers to replace it were not readily available and some repaired engines were returned to traffic with plain tanks. Ex-works 20th August 1949, No.69542 was one of them. King's Cross station.

4756

N.B. Loco. 22612.

To traffic 3/1921.

REPAIRS:
Don. 26/3—3/5/24.**G.**
Don. 2/2—16/4/26.**G.**
Don. 11/8—5/10/28.**G.**
Don. 3/3—19/4/30.**G.**
Don. 2/11/31—15/1/32.**G.**
Don. 10/11/33—13/1/34.**G.**
Don. 6/9—15/10/35.**G.**
Don. 15/6—16/7/37.**G.**
Don. 29/6—10/8/39.**G.**
Str. 3/1—23/4/43.**G.**
Don. 16/1—8/3/45.**G.**
Don. 15/8—14/10/47.**G.**
Don. 29/8—6/10/50.**G.**
Don. 30/12/52—26/1/53.**G.**
Str. 23/12/54—21/2/55.**C/L.**
Don. 30/1—10/3/56.**G.**
Don. 7—24/5/56.**C/L.**
Don. 22/9—30/10/58.**G.**

BOILERS:
7586.
7581 19/4/30.
9176 10/8/39.
8716 23/4/43.
21207 6/10/50.
21399 26/1/53.
21470 10/3/56.
21412 30/10/58.

SHEDS:
King's Cross.
Ardsley 25/4/26.
King's Cross 18/6/26.
New England 20/5/62.

RENUMBERED:
4756 3/5/24.
9535 9/11/46.
69535 6/10/50.

CONDEMNED: 16/9/62.
Into Don. for cut up 19/2/63.

4757

N.B. Loco. 22613.

To traffic 3/1921.

REPAIRS:
Don. 1—10/3/23.**L.**
Don. 17/4—24/5/24.**G.**
Don. 18/6—23/9/26.**G.**
Don. 16/8—2/11/28.**G.**
Don. 11/5—23/7/30.**G.**
Don. 16/1—5/4/32.**G.**
Don. 24/11/33—30/1/34.**G.**

Don. 24/1—15/2/36.**G.**
Str. 29/10—14/12/37.**G.**
Don. 13/7—29/8/39.**G.**
Str. 29/3—24/7/43.**G.**
Don. 2/6—26/7/46.**G.**
Don. 20/11/48—3/1/49.**G.**
Don. 16/4—15/5/51.**G.**
Don. 28/10—20/11/53.**G.**
Str. 19/2—12/6/56.**C/L.**
Don. 5/3—13/4/57.**G.**

BOILERS:
7587.
7590 2/11/28.
7597 15/2/36.
7556 14/12/37.
7589 29/8/39.
9149 26/7/46.
9141 3/1/49.
21273 15/5/51.
21230 20/11/53.
21462 13/4/57.

SHEDS:
King's Cross.
Neasden 27/10/46.
King's Cross 20/8/47.
Hitchin 1/2/59.

RENUMBERED:
4757 24/5/24.
9536 26/7/46.
69536 3/1/49.

CONDEMNED: 2/6/59.
Into Don. for cut up 2/6/59.

4758

N.B. Loco. 22614.

To traffic 3/1921.

REPAIRS:
Don. 4—25/11/22.**L.**
Don. 26/4—7/6/24.**G.**
Don. 22/6—11/10/26.**G.**
Don. 6/10—29/12/28.**G.**
Don. 14/6—13/8/30.**G.**
Don. 6/2—13/5/32.**G.**
Don. 6/11—5/1/34.**G.**
Don. 22/8—30/9/35.**G.**
Don. 2/4—26/5/37.**G.**
Don. 8/5—19/6/39.**G.**
Don. 23—29/6/39.**L.**
Don. 11/4—12/5/42.**G.**
Don. 8/3—14/4/45.**G.**
Don. 12/10—19/11/47.**G.**
Don. 13/7—13/8/48.**L.**
Don. 16/5—15/6/50.**G.**
Don. 7/12/52—2/1/53.**G.**
Don. 25/9—28/10/53.**C/L.**
Str. 7/11/55—7/1/56.**G.**

BOILERS:
7588.
7572 29/12/28.
7578 30/9/35.
9146 19/6/39.
9063 14/4/45.
8541 15/6/50.
21392 2/1/53.
21452 7/1/56.

SHEDS:
King's Cross.
Frodingham 31/5/42.
Doncaster 22/11/43.
Mexborough 18/6/44.
Hatfield 28/11/44.
Hornsey 3/1/54.

RENUMBERED:
4758 7/6/24.
9537 11/8/46.
69537 13/8/48.

CONDEMNED: 27/4/59.
Into Don. for cut up 27/4/59.

4759

N.B. Loco. 22615.

To traffic 4/1921.

REPAIRS:
Don. 13—30/12/22.**L.**
Don. 20/3—29/4/24.**G.**
Don. 16/3—19/6/26.**G.**
Don. 23/6—29/9/28.**G.**
Don. 15/5—14/7/30.**G.**
Don. 9/1—18/3/32.**G.**
Don. 8/12/33—9/2/34.**G.**
Don. 18/11—14/12/35.**G.**
Str. 4/12/37—29/1/38.**G.**
Don. 10/2—18/3/40.**G.**
Don. 3/10—6/11/43.**G.**
Don. 13/2—7/3/45.**G.**
Don. 27/4—18/6/46.**G.**
Don. 17/11—19/12/47.**G.**
Don. 16/12/49—2/2/50.**G.**
Don. 25/2—1/4/52.**C/H.**
Don. 16/1—3/3/53.**G.**
Str. 15/8—1/10/55.**G.**
Don. 2/10—13/11/58.**G.**

BOILERS:
7589.
7597 29/9/28.
7572 14/12/35.
7597 29/1/38.
9332 6/11/43.
9257 2/2/50.
21452 3/3/53.
21276 1/10/55.
21350 13/11/58.

SHEDS:
King's Cross.
Hatfield ?/?/?.
King's Cross ?/11/25.
New England 20/5/62.

RENUMBERED:
4759 29/4/24.
9538 18/6/46.
69538 2/2/50.

CONDEMNED: 16/9/62.
Into Don. for cut up 19/2/63.

4760

N.B. Loco. 22616.

To traffic 4/1921.

REPAIRS:
Don. 26/6—24/7/22.**L.**
Don. 27/2—4/4/24.**G.**
Don. 25/1—7/4/26.**G.**
Don. 13/12/27—25/2/28.**G.**
Don. 27/9—31/10/29.**G.**
Don. 29/5—19/8/31.**G.**
Don. 3/6—23/8/33.**G.**
Don. 15/2—20/3/35.**G.**
Don. 30/12/36—10/2/37.**G.**
Str. 17/11/38—12/1/39.**G.**
Don. 20/2—2/4/41.**G.**
Don. 18/5—28/6/41.**G.**
Air raid damage.
Don. 28/2—28/3/44.**G.**
Don. 11/4—7/6/46.**G.**
Don. 30/12/48—26/1/49.**G.**
Don. 8/8—1/9/50.**G.**
Don. 19/7—17/8/51.**G.**
Str. 24/11—24/12/53.**G.**
Don. 4/7—10/8/56.**G.**

BOILERS:
7590.
7680 25/2/28.
7599 31/10/29.
1368 10/2/37.
1362 28/3/44.
9176 7/6/46.
21295 17/8/51.
21477 24/12/53.
21275 10/8/56.

SHEDS:
Hatfield.
King's Cross ?/11/25.

RENUMBERED:
4760 4/4/24.
9539 17/3/46.
69539 26/1/49.

CONDEMNED: 6/7/59.
Into Don. for cut up 6/7/59.

4761

N.B. Loco. 22617.

To traffic 4/1921.

REPAIRS:
Don. 24/2—11/3/22.**L.**
Don. 20/6—20/7/22.**L.**
Don. 3/12/23—6/1/24.**G.**
Don. 4/1—9/3/26.**G.**
Don. 18/6—28/8/28.**G.**
Don. 18/1—14/3/30.**G.**
Don. 20/2—23/5/32.**G.**
Don. 8/12/33—15/2/34.**G.**
Don. 18/6—11/7/36.**G.**
Don. 4/8—13/9/38.**G.**
Don. 1/2—4/4/41.**G.**
Don. 6/4—6/5/44.**G.**
Don. 8/3—6/4/46.**G.**
Don. 5/6—7/8/47.**G.**
Don. 26/6—11/8/49.**C/H.**
Don. 4/8—3/9/51.**G.**
Str. 9/2—2/4/54.**G.**
Don. 29/12/56—2/2/57.**G.**
Don. 4—5/2/57.**N/C.**

BOILERS:
7591.
7681 9/3/26.
8993 11/7/36.
8995 13/9/38.
9778 7/8/47.
21302 3/9/51.
21409 2/4/54.
21243 2/2/57.

SHEDS:
Hatfield.
King's Cross ?/11/25.
Hitchin 1/2/59.
New England 14/6/59.

RENUMBERED:
1761ɴ 6/1/24.
4761 9/3/26.
9540 5/4/46.
69540 11/8/49.

CONDEMNED: 21/7/60.
Into Don. for cut up 21/7/60.

4762

N.B. Loco. 22618.

To traffic 4/1921.

REPAIRS:
Don. 4—8/4/22.**L.**
Don. 20/3—10/5/24.**G.**
Don. 15/4—6/8/26.**G.**
Don. 3/1—17/3/28.**G.**
Don. 27/9—30/10/29.**G.**

Don. 4/7—2/9/31.**G.**
Don. 25/3—1/7/33.**G.**
T.A.B. valves fitted.
Don. 29/10—22/12/34.**G.**
Str. 13/10—18/11/36.**G.**
Don. 19/2—14/4/39.**G.**
Don. 22/8—24/9/41.**G.**
Don. 13/8—6/9/44.**G.**
Don. 4/11—11/12/47.**G.**
Don. 12/9—12/10/50.**G.**
Don. 23/4—21/5/53.**G.**
Str. 19/6—16/8/56.**G.**

BOILERS:
7592.
7573 17/3/28.
7595 30/10/29.
7592 22/12/34.
8996 18/11/36.
9143 14/4/39.
9265 11/12/47.
21206 12/10/50.
21462 21/5/53.
21251 16/8/56.

SHEDS:
Hatfield.
King's Cross ?/11/25.
Hornsey 29/9/57.
King's Cross 24/11/57.

RENUMBERED:
4762 10/5/24.
9541 31/8/46.
69541 12/10/50.

CONDEMNED: 6/8/59.
Into Don. for cut up 6/8/59.

4763

N.B. Loco. 22619.

To traffic 4/1921.

REPAIRS:
Don. 12/10/23—19/1/24.**G.**
Don. 2/7—15/8/25.**G.**
Don. 16/5—22/7/27.**G.**
Don. 8/3—14/5/29.**G.**
Don. 31/1—9/4/31.**G.**
Don. 25/11/32—21/2/33.**G.**
Rail washing apparatus fitted.
Don. 29/9—2/11/34.**G.**
Str. 2/10—6/11/36.**G.**
Str. 7/12/38—23/2/39.**G.**
Str. 15/5—28/6/41.**G.**
Str. 22/1—10/2/43.**L.**
Slidebar bracket broken.
Don. 20/6—29/7/44.**G.**
Don. 16/10—16/11/46.**G.**
Don. 10/7—20/8/49.**G.**
Don. 3—31/10/51.**G.**
Str. 15/2—19/3/54.**G.**

Str. 28/4—5/5/54.**N/C.**
Don. 8/8—8/9/56.**G.**
Don. 12—18/9/56.**N/C.**

BOILERS:
7593.
7679 22/7/27.
7544 2/11/34.
7680 6/11/36.
7563 23/2/39.
1372 28/6/41.
9621 16/11/46.
21315 31/10/51.
21408 19/3/54.
21429 *(new)* 8/9/56.

SHEDS:
Hatfield.
King's Cross 20/1/24.
Neasden 5/11/43.
King's Cross 21/4/44.

RENUMBERED:
1763ɴ 19/1/24.
4763 ?/3/25.
9542 2/11/46.
69542 20/8/49.

CONDEMNED: 6/4/59.
Into Don. for cut up 6/4/59.

4764

N.B. Loco. 22620.

To traffic 4/1921.

REPAIRS:
Don. 1/4—10/5/24.**G.**
Don. 27/4—6/8/26.**G.**
Don. 21/2—4/5/28.**G.**
Don. 16/11—31/12/29.**G.**
Don. 2/10—26/11/31.**G.**
Don. 4/8—29/9/33.**G.**
Don. 11/7—17/8/35.**G.**
Don. 29/8—6/9/35.**L.**
Don. 18/4—5/6/37.**G.**
Don. 1/8—23/9/39.**G.**
Str. 15/3—11/9/43.**G.**
Don. 22/3—11/5/46.**G.**
Don. 31/10—9/12/48.**G.**
Don. 27/7—24/8/51.**G.**
Str. 2/3—1/5/54.**G.**
Str. 26/7—21/9/57.**G.**

BOILERS:
7594.
7581 4/5/28.
7573 31/12/29.
7571 26/11/31.
9179 23/9/39.
9148 11/5/46.
21299 24/8/51.
21302 1/5/54.

21281 21/9/57.

SHEDS:
Hitchin.
King's Cross 20/1/24.
Hornsey 25/9/60.
New England 9/7/61.

RENUMBERED:
4764 10/5/24.
9543 11/5/46.
69543 9/12/48.

CONDEMNED: 11/9/61.
Into Don. for cut up 11/9/61.

4765

N.B. Loco. 22621.

To traffic 4/1921.

REPAIRS:
Don. 20/3—19/4/24.**G.**
Don. 24/3—24/6/26.**G.**
Don. 11/9—8/12/28.**G.**
Don. 10/10—4/12/30.**G.**
Don. 23/7—11/10/32.**G.**
Don. 8/2—7/3/35.**G.**
Don. 8/11/36—2/1/37.**G.**
Str. 1/12/38—27/1/39.**G.**
Don. 11/5—13/6/41.**G.**
Don. 15/7—12/8/44.**G.**
Don. 6/8—24/9/47.**G.**
Don. 25/7—25/8/50.**G.**
Don. 25/2—9/4/52.**C/L.**
Don. 1—28/5/53.**G.**
Don. 22/12/55—28/1/56.**G.**
Don. 5/12/58. *Not repaired.*

BOILERS:
7595.
7594 8/12/28.
7679 7/3/35.
8284 2/1/37.
8283 27/1/39.
9267 13/6/41.
9070 25/8/50.
21231 28/5/53.

SHED:
King's Cross.

RENUMBERED:
4765 19/4/24.
9544 30/10/46.
69544 25/8/50.

CONDEMNED: 8/12/58.
Cut up at Doncaster.

(right) **Until the end of 1925, GNR parallel case buffers were standard fitting but the subsequent twenty-nine built had Group Standard type with stepped case and square flange (*see* page 44, bottom). Bradford shed, 7th July 1935.**

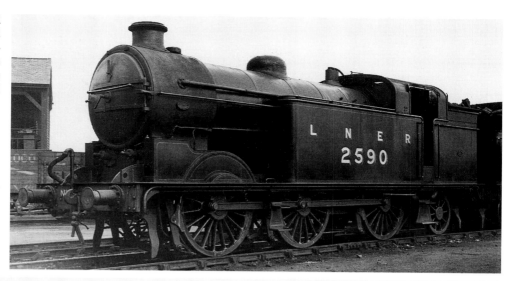

(below) **Of those with GN buffers only No.69523 (ex 4744) has been traced as changed to GS type. They were fitted ex-works 17th March 1950 following a collision at Welwyn G.C. with V2 class 60850 on 2nd January 1950. Wood Green, June 1959.**

(below) **The driving coupled axleboxes had helical springs and the leading and trailing boxes had laminated type. Only one change was made; ex-works 13th May 1953, No. 69579 had the helical springs replaced by laminated type. Riding was better but plate breakage was frequent so no more were altered. Hornsey shed, July 1960.**

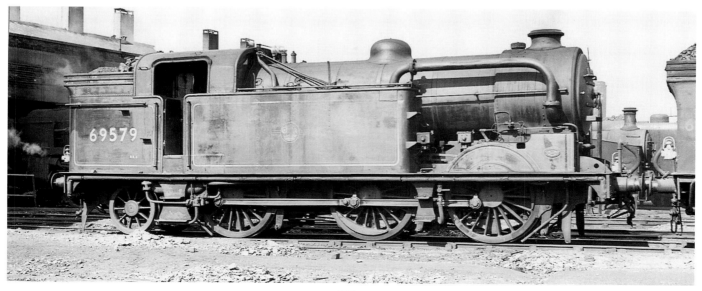

(left) **As built, all one hundred and seven had two open coal rails on top of the sides and rear of the bunker (*see* page 45, middle). King's Cross shed, 5th July 1931.**

(below) **Engines working in the Scottish Area needed to have the top rail taken off to suit their coal stage working position.**

When such engines were sent or returned to Southern Area, Doncaster usually took the first opportunity of restoring the second rail.

4766

N.B. Loco. 22622.

To traffic 4/1921.

REPAIRS:
Don. 22/3—7/4/23.**L.**
Don. 26/4—31/5/24.**G.**
Don. 12/8—18/11/26.**G.**
Don. 3/11/28—29/3/29.**G.**
Don. 25/1—26/3/31.**G.**
Don. 8/10—7/12/32.**G.**
Gor. 29/6—18/8/34.**G.**
Gor. 23/7—26/8/36.**G.**
Str. 21/6—6/8/38.**G.**
T.A.B. valves fitted.
Don. 30/5—29/6/40.**G.**
Don. 8/12/43—6/1/44.**G.**
Don. 9/4—7/6/46.**G.**
Don. 11/12/46—25/1/47.**L.**
Don. 7—28/11/47.**L.**
Don. 7/11—15/12/48.**G.**
Don. 6/5—4/6/51.**G.**
Don. 12/10—25/11/53.**G.**
Don. 18/9—12/10/56.**G.**

BOILERS:
7596.
7589 18/11/26.
7588 29/3/29.
8995 26/8/36.
8104 6/8/38.
7680 7/6/46.
8711 15/12/48.
21278 4/6/51.
21273 25/11/53.
21239 12/10/56.

SHEDS:
King's Cross.
Neasden 27/10/46.
King's Cross 14/5/47.

RENUMBERED:
4766 31/5/24.
9545 7/6/46.
69545 15/12/48.

CONDEMNED: 20/7/59.
Into Don. for cut up 20/7/59.

4767

N.B. Loco. 22623.

To traffic 4/1921.

REPAIRS:
Don. 7/12/23—26/1/24.**G.**
Kx. 7/2—16/3/25.**L.**
Don. 30/9—14/11/25.**G.**
Don. 19/11/27—9/2/28.**G.**
Ashcroft cut-off control fitted.

Don. 14/9—26/10/29.**G.**
Don. 26/6—31/8/31.**G.**
T.A.B. valves fitted.
Don. 9/4—13/6/32.**L.**
Don. 27/10—22/12/33.**G.**
Don. 22/6—31/7/35.**G.**
Don. 24/7—20/8/37.**G.**
Don. 2/7—25/8/39.**G.**
Don. 10/8—17/9/41.**G.**
Don. 18/10—15/11/44.**G.**
Don. 27/11/47—2/1/48.**G.**
Don. 18/8—28/9/50.**G.**
Don. 9/5—5/6/53.**G.**
Str. 5/12/55—15/2/56.**G.**
Str. 15/4—22/6/56.**C/L.**
Don. 4/4—12/5/59.**G.**

BOILERS:
7597.
7593 9/2/28.
7592 25/8/39.
9325 15/11/44.
21203 28/9/50.
21206 5/6/53.
21387 15/2/56.
21459 12/5/59.

SHEDS:
King's Cross.
New England 10/9/61.

RENUMBERED:
1767N 26/1/24.
4767 16/3/25.
9546 1/11/46.
69546 28/9/50.

CONDEMNED: 23/9/62.
Into Don. for cut up 21/2/63.

4768

N.B. Loco. 22624.

To traffic 4/1921.

REPAIRS:
Don. 2—27/5/22.**L.**
Don. 17/4—31/5/24.**G.**
Don. 27/8—30/11/26.**G.**
Don. 22/10—27/4/29.**G.**
Don. 4/7—3/9/31.**G.**
Don. 29/6—7/9/33.**G.**
Don. 14/6—26/7/35.**G.**
Don. 30/4—2/7/37.**G.**
Don. 31/12/39—29/1/40.**G.**
Don. 9/10—21/11/40.**G.**
Air raid damage.
Don. 28/12/43—22/1/44.**G.**
Str. 8/11/46—19/3/47.**G.**
Don. 13/9—7/11/49.**G.**
Don. 13/9—19/10/51.**G.**
Str. 3/5—19/6/54.**G.**
Str. 15/9—9/11/57.**G.**

BOILERS:
7598.
7583 27/4/29.
7587 26/7/35.
7578 29/1/40.
9223 21/11/40.
8837 19/3/47.
8139 7/11/49.
21311 19/10/51.
21299 19/6/54.

SHEDS:
Hornsey.
Hatfield 14/11/55.

RENUMBERED:
4768 31/5/24.
9547 3/11/46.
69547 5/11/49.

CONDEMNED: 10/6/59.
Into Don. for cut up 10/6/59.

4769

N.B. Loco. 22625.

To traffic 4/1921.

REPAIRS:
Don. 19/4—5/5/23.**L.**
Don. 30/4—14/6/24.**G.**
Don. 27/8—1/12/26.**G.**
Don. 20/10/28—8/2/29.**G.**
Don. 15/9—17/11/30.**G.**
Don. 25/6—23/9/32.**G.**
Gor. 26/5—21/7/34.**G.**
Str. 3/1—4/3/37.**G.**
Don. 19/6—21/7/39.**G.**
Don. 13/3—26/4/42.**G.**
Don. 14/2—23/3/46.**G.**
Don. 27/8—11/10/48.**G.**
Don. 8/2—6/3/51.**G.**
Don. 28/8—5/10/53.**G.**
Don. 12/7—16/8/56.**G.**

BOILERS:
7599.
7563 8/2/29.
7580 21/7/34.
7567 4/3/37.
9148 21/7/39.
8985 23/3/46.
21243 6/3/51.
21238 5/10/53.
21477 16/8/56.

SHEDS:
King's Cross.
Doncaster 2/5/42.
Mexborough 9/5/42.
Hitchin 30/4/44.
King's Cross 28/4/46.
Hornsey 6/10/57.

King's Cross 24/11/57.
New England 7/12/58.
Hitchin 1/2/59.

RENUMBERED:
4769 14/6/24.
9548 23/3/46.
69548 9/10/48.

CONDEMNED: 24/7/59.
Into Don. for cut up 24/7/59.

4770

N.B. Loco. 22626.

To traffic 4/1921.

REPAIRS:
Don. 30/1—10/2/23.**L.**
Don. 26/4—7/6/24.**G.**
Don. 30/12/26—17/3/27.**G.**
Don. 27/10—8/2/29.**G.**
Don. 1—16/3/29.**N/C.**
Don. 23/2—26/5/31.**G.**
Don. 16/12/32—22/2/33.**G.**
Don. 25/1—28/2/35.**G.**
Don. 8/11—18/12/36.**G.**
Str. 23/11/38—16/1/39.**G.**
Don. 10/11/40—11/1/41.**G.**
Cracked tubeplate.
Don. 17/1—18/2/44.**G.**
Don. 9/8—16/10/46.**G.**
Don. 19/2—18/3/49.**G.**
Don. 18/10—9/11/51.**G.**
Str. 15/9—22/10/54.**G.**
Don. 1/7—10/8/57.**G.**
Don. 14—15/8/57.**N/C.**
Don. 31/7—15/8/58.**C/L.**

BOILERS:
7600.
7587 8/2/29.
7539 28/2/35.
1372 18/12/36.
9224 11/1/41.
10522 18/3/49.
21319 9/11/51.
21402 22/10/54.
21301 10/8/57.

SHEDS:
King's Cross.
Hatfield 5/10/42.
King's Cross 19/12/43.
Grantham 29/5/60.
New England 21/5/61.

RENUMBERED:
4770 7/6/24.
9549 16/10/46.
69549 26/2/49.

(left) **From the early 1930's plating was put behind the coal rail or rails to help prevent spillage of small coal. Parkhead shed, June 1935.**

(below) **The introduction of mechanical coaling plants enabled those Scottish engines served by them to have extra coal capacity provided by two rails. Parkhead shed, 3rd August 1958.**

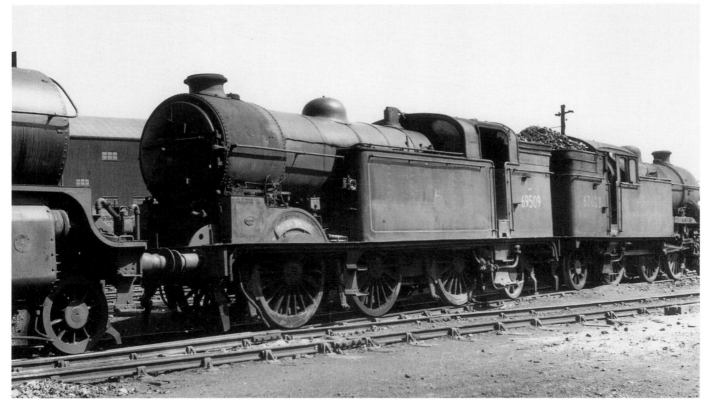

By no means did all the Scottish N2's have the second coal rail put on and some still had only one to withdrawal. Parkhead shed, 17th May 1953.

From June 1931 a backing plate was fitted all round the bunker but London crews complained they interfered with the view when running in reverse. This was agreed and from April 1932 only the side rails had plating. King's Cross shed, 30th April 1958.

On the fireman's side, two steps were fitted on the bunker and there was an angled hand-grip at the edge of the cab roof to aid access to the top of the bunker. Nos.2583 to 2594 were fitted similarly but on the right hand side, as they had left hand drive. Carlisle Canal shed, 29th March 1937.

In error, Doncaster fitted these steps onto Nos.892 to 897 on the left hand side as they had done on Nos.4606 to 4615, overlooking that the driving position had been changed. The steps remained on the driver's side (*see* page 109, top).

4770 cont./
CONDEMNED: 12/9/61.
Into Don. for cut up 12/9/61.

2583

Beyer Peacock 6210.

To traffic 28/2/25.

REPAIRS:
Gor. 14/3/25.**L***.
Gor. 21/3/25.**L***.
Gor. 28/3/25.**L***.
Gor. 11—18/4/25.**L***.
Gor. 25/4—2/5/25.**L***.
*All for hot boxes.
Cow. 5—25/11/25.**L**.
Cow. 21/11—25/12/25.**L**.
Cow. 21/11/27—10/1/28.**G**.
Cow. 24/10/30—31/1/31.**G**.
Don. 19/4—19/7/33.**G**.
Don. 24/10—28/11/35.**G**.
Don. 19/11—11/12/37.**G**.
Don. 20/5—18/6/40.**G**.
Don. 21/3—22/4/44.**G**.
Don. 5/7—31/8/46.**G**.
Don. 10/5—2/6/49.**G**.
Don. 3/4—2/5/52.**G**.
Don. 3—16/1/53.**C/L**.
Don. 13/5—30/6/53.**C/L**.
Str. 22/8—4/11/55.**G**.

BOILERS:
1362.
8138 28/11/35.
1370 31/8/46.
9149 2/6/49.
21350 2/5/52.
21358 4/11/55.

SHEDS:
Gorton.
Eastfield 13/5/25.
Burnbank (Hamilton)
by 28/11/25.
Eastfield ?/?/?.
Kipps 30/11/26.
Eastfield 6/3/30.
Ardsley 5/2/31.
Bradford 14/2/31.
King's Cross 23/9/41.
Hitchin 9/12/41.
Mexborough 30/4/44.
Colwick 7/4/46.
King's Cross 22/4/51.
Hatfield 29/4/51.
Stratford 14/9/52.
Colchester 21/9/52.
Stratford 15/3/53.
King's Cross 14/10/56.
Hornsey 30/6/57.

RENUMBERED:
9550 28/7/46.
69550 2/6/49.

CONDEMNED: 2/9/58.
Into Don. for cut up 2/8/58.

2584

Beyer Peacock 6211.

To traffic 17/2/25.

REPAIRS:
Cow. 12—28/11/25.**L**.
Cow. 19—23/4/27.**L**.
Cow. 29/10—14/12/27.**G**.
Cow. 18/1—9/2/28.**L**.
Cow. 29/2—14/3/28.**N/C**.
Cow. 7/8—6/9/28.**N/C**.
Cow. 11/9—9/10/28.**N/C**.
Cow. 20/11—5/12/28.**L**.
Cow. 25—31/7/29.**N/C**.
Cow. 21/8—13/9/29.**L**.
Cow. 17/10—2/11/29.**N/C**.
Cow. 20/11—14/12/29.**L**.
Cow. 25/11/30—29/1/31.**G**.
Don. 30/8—13/10/33.**G**.
Don. 26/11—27/12/35.**G**.
Don. 5—28/1/38.**G**.
Don. 28/7—24/8/40.**G**.
Don. 30/11/43—5/1/44.**G**.
Don. 7/3—14/4/45.**G**.
Don. 6—31/10/47.**G**.
Don. 10/8—4/10/49.**G**.
Don. 7/1—1/2/52.**G**.
Don. 6/7—13/8/53.**C/L**.
Str. 15/9—23/10/54.**G**.

BOILERS:
1363.
9064 28/1/38.
8097 14/4/45.
8139 31/10/47.
9337 4/10/49.
21336 1/2/52.
21413 23/10/54.

SHEDS:
Gorton.
Dundee 27/2/25.
Eastfield 28/11/25.
Kipps 30/11/26.
Ardsley 26/2/31.
Bradford 3/3/31.
Copley Hill 8/5/37.
Bradford 27/3/41.
King's Cross 23/9/41.
Hornsey 27/9/41.
Hitchin 9/12/41.
Hatfield 12/7/42.
Stratford 20/7/52.
Parkeston 27/7/52.

King's Cross 28/10/56.
Hornsey 23/6/57.

RENUMBERED:
9551 28/7/46.
69551 4/10/49.

CONDEMNED: 3/12/58.
Into Don. for cut up 3/12/58.

2585

Beyer Peacock 6212.

To traffic 27/2/25.

REPAIRS:
Cow. 4/7—27/8/27.**G**.
Cow. 11/9—12/10/29.**G**.
Cow. 13/2—28/3/31.**G**.
Cow. 1/4—15/5/31.**L**.
Don. 27/2—3/4/35.**G**.
Don. 22/2—25/3/37.**G**.
Don. 6/3—15/4/39.**G**.
Don. 9/11/41—1/1/42.**G**.
Don. 27/10—18/11/44.**G**.
Don. 22/1—1/3/47.**G**.
Don. 4/4—5/5/49.**G**.
Don. 12/9—23/11/50.**H/I**.
Don. 6/2—13/3/53.**G**.
Don. 11/6—22/7/53.**C/L**.
Str. 6/2—24/3/56.**G**.
Don. 27/4/60. *Not repaired.*

BOILERS:
1364.
9147 15/4/39.
8563 18/11/44.
8563 reno.21225 23/11/50.
21209 13/3/53.
21310 24/3/56.

SHEDS:
Gorton.
Dundee 5/3/25.
Haymarket 26/3/30.
Ardsley 27/5/31.
Bradford 12/12/37.
Copley Hill 30/5/38.
Bradford 29/7/38.
Doncaster 2/11/41.
King's Cross 29/11/41.
Hornsey 7/12/41.
King's Cross 16/6/42.
Hatfield 2/10/42.
Mexborough 20/11/44.
Colwick 13/3/46.
Hatfield 6/5/51.
King's Cross 18/5/52.
Parkeston 3/8/52.
King's Cross 28/10/56.
Hornsey 23/6/57.
Grantham 16/11/58.

RENUMBERED:
9552 4/8/46.
69552 5/5/49.

CONDEMNED: 9/5/60.
Cut up at Doncaster.

2586

Beyer Peacock 6213.

To traffic 28/2/25.

REPAIRS:
Cow. ?/?—?/11/27.**G**.
(Cowlairs records missing).
Cow. 14/1—14/2/31.**G**.
Cow. ?/6—17/6/33.**G**.
Cow. ?/?—7/12/34.**L**.
Cow. ?/?—15/8/35.**G**.
Cow. ?/?—1/5/37.**G**.
Cow. 2—23/9/39.**G**.
Cow. ?/?—17/5/41.**L**.
Cow. ?/?—25/1/42.**L**.
Cow. ?/?—4/6/42.**L**.
Cow. ?/?—19/9/42.**L**.
Cow. ?/?—9/10/42.**L**.
Cow. ?/?—20/3/43.**G**.
Cow. 2—16/9/44.**G**.
Cow. 12—20/1/45.**L**.
Cow. ?/?—6/11/46.**N/C**.
Cow. 12/12/47—21/2/48.**G**.
Cow. ?/?—4/6/49.**C/L**.
Cow. ?/?—13/5/50.**C/L**.
Cow. 1/10—1/11/52.**G**.
Cow. 12—20/12/52.**C/L**.
Cow. 11/8/54.**N/C**.
Cow. 13/9—9/10/54.**L/I**.
Cow. 6—10/12/54.**N/C**.
Cow. 26—30/4/55.**N/C**.
Cow. 6—7/4/56.**N/C**.
Cow. 3—11/1/58.**C/L**.

BOILERS:
1365.
C1681 *(ex4739)* 17/6/33.
C1670 *(ex4724)* 23/9/39.
1365 *(ex4731)* 16/9/44.
C1708 *(ex9509)* 21/2/48.
21531 *(ex69510)* 1/11/52.

SHEDS:
Gorton.
St Margarets 6/3/25.
Hatfield 12/3/31.
Cambridge 20/1/32.
Stratford 8/2/32.
Hatfield 26/4/32.
Kipps 18/11/32.
Parkhead 20/6/48.
Kipps 23/9/51.
Parkhead 14/4/52.
Dawsholm 12/5/52.

2586 cont./
RENUMBERED:
9553 30/6/46.
69553 4/6/49.

CONDEMNED: 3/12/59.
Cut up at Cowlairs 20/2/60.

2587

Beyer Peacock 6214.

To traffic 10/3/25.

REPAIRS:
Cow. 18/8—6/10/27.**G.**
Cow. 13/2—10/4/29.**G.**
Cow. 11/6—25/7/31.**G.**
Ghd. 28/8—7/9/31.**N/C.**
Don. 5/10—12/11/31.**L.**
Don. 16/9—8/12/32.**G.**
Don. 17/8—8/10/35.**G.**
Don. 30/8—7/10/37.**G.**
Don. 24/8—11/10/39.**G.**
Don. 9/10—8/11/41.**L.**
Str. 22/8—12/11/42.**G.**
Don. 10/6—17/7/43.**H.**
Don. 24/3—18/5/45.**G.**
Don. 2/6—10/8/47.**G.**
Don. 3/8—21/9/50.**G.**
Don. 28/5—30/6/53.**G.**

BOILERS:
1366.
8095 7/10/37.
9328 17/7/43.
9142 10/8/47.
21201 21/9/50.
21465 30/6/53.

SHEDS:
Gorton.
St Margarets 18/3/25.
Ardsley 27/7/31.
Bradford 10/9/31.
Doncaster 19/10/41.
King's Cross 29/11/41.
Hatfield 7/12/41.
King's Cross 2/8/53.
Hatfield 17/1/54.
Hornsey 14/11/55.

RENUMBERED:
9554 28/7/46.
69554 21/9/50.

CONDEMNED: 10/6/58.
Into Don. for cut up 10/6/58.

2588

Beyer Peacock 6215.

To traffic 2/3/25.

REPAIRS:
Cow. 24/11—14/12/26.**L.**
Cow. 22/12/27—3/2/28.**G.**
Cow. 26/12/29—15/2/30.**G.**
Cow. 17/11—28/12/31.**G.**
Don. 29/12/31—1/3/32.**N/C.**
Condensing and trip cock gear fitted.
Don. 12/1—10/4/34.**G.**
Don. 5/4—9/5/36.**G.**
Str. 28/3—19/5/38.**G.**
Don. 3/11/40—1/1/41.**G.**
Don. 11—13/6/42.**N/C.**
Don. 18/7—18/8/44.**G.**
Don. 7—14/10/44.**N/C.**
Don. 25/11/46—25/1/47.**G.**
Don. 9/11—23/12/48.**G.**
Don. 11/5—8/6/51.**G.**
Don. 13/9—9/10/53.**G.**
Don. 3/4/59. *Not repaired.*

BOILERS:
1367.
7552 10/4/34.
8091 19/5/38.
8699 18/8/44.
21281 8/6/51.
21252 9/10/53.

SHEDS:
Gorton.
St Margarets 10/3/25.
Burnbank (Hamilton) 4/2/26.
Eastfield 20/12/28.
Carlisle Canal 29/10/30.
King's Cross 29/12/31.
Hornsey 9/3/32.
Doncaster 9/6/42.
Mexborough 20/6/42.
Doncaster 18/6/44.
Mexborough 17/9/44.
Colwick 13/3/46.
King's Cross 22/4/51.
Hatfield 29/4/51.
Stratford 14/9/52.
Colchester 21/9/52.
Hornsey 20/11/55.
Colchester 25/12/55.
King's Cross 14/10/56.
Hornsey 7/4/57.

RENUMBERED:
9555 28/7/46.
69555 23/12/48.

CONDEMNED: 6/4/59.
Cut up at Doncaster.

2589

Beyer Peacock 6216.

To traffic 4/3/25.

REPAIRS:
Cow. 31/8—8/12/26.**G.**
Cow. 20—26/4/27.**N/C.**
Cow. 6—17/9/27.**L.**
Cow. 31/10—13/12/28.**G.**
Cow. 5/6—5/7/29.**L.**
Cow. 9/10—2/12/30.**G.**
Don. 22/4—16/8/32.**G.**
Condensing and trip cock gear fitted.
Don. 24/8—2/10/34.**G.**
Str. 5/10—20/11/36.**G.**
Don. 24/1—16/3/39.**G.**
Don. 14/8—8/10/43.**G.**
Don. 17/8—11/10/46.**G.**
Don. 13/3—6/5/49.**G.**
Don. 19/11—14/12/51.**G.**
Str. 27/4—5/6/54.**G.**
Don. 7/10—9/11/56.**G.**

BOILERS:
1368.
1367 20/11/36.
9140 16/3/39.
9225 11/10/46.
10525 6/5/49.
21329 14/12/51.
21271 5/6/54.
21273 9/11/56.

SHEDS:
Gorton.
St Margarets 17/3/25.
Parkhead 6/2/26.
Kipps 30/5/28.
Hatfield 8/12/30.
Hornsey 25/11/32.

RENUMBERED:
9556 21/7/46.
69556 6/5/49.

CONDEMNED: 18/12/59.
Into Str. for cut up 18/12/59.

2590

Beyer Peacock 6217.

To traffic 12/3/25.

REPAIRS:
Gor. 21—28/3/25.**L.**
Cow. 3—24/4/26.**L.**
Cow. 20/7—7/9/27.**G.**
Cow. 21/8—26/9/28.**G.**
Cow. 29/1—8/3/30.**G.**
Cow. 11—22/3/30.**N/C.**
Cow. 28/3—9/4/30.**N/C.**
Cow. 4/11—15/12/31.**G.**
Gor. 3/4—2/6/34.**G.**
Don. 24/9—17/10/36.**G.**
Don. 30/12/38—25/1/39.**G.**
Don. 9/9—9/10/40.**G.**
Don. 18/7—18/8/41.**L.**
Firebox tubeplate fractured.
Don. 29/1—24/2/44.**G.**
Don. 1/2—2/3/48.**G.**
Don. 22/3—26/4/49.**C/L.**
Don. 7/3—10/4/52.**G.**
Don. 30/9—27/10/52.**C/L.**
Str. 31/8—27/10/54.**C/L.**

BOILERS:
1369.
8101 17/10/36.
9143 2/3/48.
21410 10/4/52.

SHEDS:
Gorton.
Dundee 9/4/25.
Hawick 28/9/28.
St Margarets 22/10/30.
Bradford 15/12/31.
Copley Hill 29/7/37.
Ardsley 2/12/39.
Bradford 26/3/41.
Hitchin 3/11/41.
Doncaster 9/6/42.
Mexborough 20/6/42.
Hornsey 1/4/46.
Hitchin 7/8/46.

RENUMBERED:
9557 21/7/46.
ᴇ9557 2/3/48.
69557 26/4/49.

CONDEMNED: 17/6/57.
Into Don. for cut up 17/6/57.

2591

Beyer Peacock 6218.

To traffic 14/3/25.

REPAIRS:
Cow. 2/4—18/5/27.**G.**
Cow. 20/2—6/4/29.**G.**

WORKS CODES:- Bpk - Beyer, Peacock. Cw - Cowlairs. Dar- Darlington. Don - Doncaster. Ghd - Gateshead. Gor - Gorton. Inv - Inverurie. Str - Stratford.
REPAIR CODES:- **C/H** - Casual Heavy. **C/L** - Casual Light. **G** - General. **H**- Heavy. **H/I** - Heavy Intermediate. **L** - Light. **L/I** - Light Intermediate. **N/C** - Non-Classified.

81

Although the bunker steps remained, a number lost the hand grip in later years. Kipps shed, 1st August 1958.

At first Nos. 4606 to 4615 and 4721 to 4770 had only a small plate on the front of the tank to act as a footstep.

From 1932 a more substantial step was substituted and from 1939 both tank fronts were similarly equipped. King's Cross station, 1938.

Where no Westinghouse pump or mechanical lubricator prevented it, a second step on the tank front was put on. Doncaster works.

For use on suburban trains in London District, engines working there had brackets on the back of the bunker for destination boards. At the front the destination board brackets were on the smokebox door. Hadley Wood, September 1946.

The GRANGE PARK headboard, along with other boards, fixed in the brackets at the front of No.4768. The widespread use of this class in the London area made it prone to bomb damage during the 1939-45 war. This is how 4768 of Hornsey shed arrived at Doncaster works on 9th October 1940, peppered by splinters, but no N2 had any really significant damage or were out of action for longer than a normal general repair period. 4768 was back to traffic on 21st November 1940.

2591 cont./
Cow. 19/5—24/6/31.**G.**
Don. 9/2—22/4/33.**G.**
Don. 30/12/35—17/1/36.**G.**
Don. 2—25/2/38.**G.**
Don. 24/4—24/5/40.**G.**
Don. 12—13/8/41.*Weigh.*
Don. 19/5—25/6/43.**G.**
Don. 6/1—16/2/46.**G.**
Don. 12/5—18/6/48.**G.**
Don. 17/9—13/10/50.**G.**
Don. 7/8—2/9/53.**G.**

BOILERS:
1370.
1362 17/1/36.
1366 25/2/38.
8283 25/6/43.
9222 18/6/48.
21405 *(new)* 13/10/50.
21263 2/9/53.

SHEDS:
Gorton.
Dundee 25/3/25.
Haymarket 30/10/30.
St Margarets 2/12/30.
Haymarket 27/2/31.
Ardsley 25/6/31.
Copley Hill 10/12/37.
Ardsley 6/4/41.
King's Cross 10/9/41.
Hatfield 14/9/41.
Stratford 14/9/52.
Colchester 22/9/52.
King's Cross 19/8/56.

RENUMBERED:
9558 28/7/46.
69558 18/6/48.

*CONDEMNED:*3/6/57.
Into Don. for cut up 3/6/57.

2592

Beyer Peacock 6219.

To traffic 18/3/25.

REPAIRS:
Cow. 8/9—18/10/27.**G.**
Cow. 11/2—8/3/30.**G.**
Cow. 15/10—15/12/31.**G.**
Don. 27/2—26/4/34.**G.**
Don. 14/9—3/10/36.**G.**
Don. 12/7—12/8/38.**G.**
Don. 4/9—28/11/40.**G.**
Don. 12—13/8/41.*Weigh.*
Don. 8—30/11/43.**G.**
Don. 11/4—23/5/45.**G.**
Don. 11/7—18/8/45.**L.**
Don. 2/2—16/3/48.**G.**
Don. 20/3—27/4/50.**G.**

Str. 14/2—20/2/52.**N/C.**
Don. 28/9—28/10/52.**G.**

BOILERS:
1371.
8997 3/10/36.
8096 12/8/38.
9064 23/5/45.
9791 16/3/48.
9326 27/4/50.
21381 28/10/52.

SHEDS:
Gorton.
Dundee 27/3/25.
Haymarket 30/5/31.
Ardsley 15/12/31.
Copley Hill 11/12/37.
Bradford 27/3/41.
King's Cross 23/9/41.
Hatfield 7/12/41.
Stratford 20/7/52.
Parkeston 27/7/52.
Stratford 3/8/52.
King's Cross 19/8/56.

RENUMBERED:
9559 28/7/46.
ᴇ9559 16/3/48.
69559 27/4/50.

CONDEMNED: 18/7/57.
Into Don. for cut up 18/7/57.

2593

Beyer Peacock 6220.

To traffic 21/3/25.

REPAIRS:
Gor. 11—18/4/25.**L.**
Cow. 1/6—9/7/27.**L.**
Cow. 2/12/27—28/1/28.**G.**
Cow. 26/3—10/5/28.**L.**
Cow. 11/3—8/5/31.**G.**
Don. 27/10—8/12/33.**G.**
Don. 25/5—27/6/36.**G.**
Don. 16/5—15/6/38.**G.**
Don. 6—31/8/40.**G.**
Don. 9/10—29/11/42.**G.**
Don. 27/8—29/9/45.**G.**
Don. 28/10—14/12/48.**G.**
Don. 19/11—19/12/53.**G.**
Str. 17/5—26/7/57.**G.**

BOILERS:
1372.
8096 27/6/36.
8092 15/6/38.
9330 29/11/42.
8133 14/12/48.
21213 19/12/53.

SHEDS:
Gorton.
Eastfield 17/4/25.
Dundee 20/2/29.
Ardsley 9/5/31.
Hatfield 3/11/41.
Mexborough 6/12/42.
Neasden 17/11/43.
King's Cross 27/10/46.
Colwick 22/6/47.
Woodford 26/2/50.
Hatfield 29/4/51.
King's Cross 9/9/51.
Hornsey 19/10/52.
Grantham 14/6/59.

RENUMBERED:
9560 28/7/46.
69560 14/12/48.

CONDEMNED: 18/10/60.
Into Don. for cut up 18/10/60.

2594

Beyer Peacock 6221.

To traffic 26/3/25.

REPAIRS:
Cow. 9/12/27—17/2/28.**G.**
Cow. 5/6—3/7/29.**G.**
Cow. 4/11/31—26/1/32.**G.**
Ghd. 3—10/2/32.**N/C.**
Gor. 25/5—21/7/34.**G.**
Don. 11/1—6/2/37.**G.**
Don. 2/3—6/5/39.**G.**
Don. 18/9—1/11/41.**G.**
Don. 29/7—7/8/43.**L.**
Don. 31/10—29/11/44.**G.**
Don. 10/6—19/7/47.**G.**
Don. 13/1—23/2/50.**G.**
Don. 2/6—9/7/53.**G.**
Str. 20/10—11/11/55.**C/L.**
Str. 25/4—7/6/56.**G.**

BOILERS:
1373.
1371 6/2/37.
9175 6/5/39.
8993 19/7/47.
10556 23/2/50.
21466 9/7/53.
21209 7/6/56.

SHEDS:
Gorton.
Eastfield 17/4/25.
Haymarket 10/5/29.
Eastfield 3/7/29.
Hawick 11/3/30.
Kipps 31/1/31.
Ardsley 26/1/32.
Doncaster 2/11/41.

King's Cross 29/11/41.
Hitchin 7/12/41.
Doncaster 2/5/42.
Mexborough 9/5/42.
Neasden 2/2/44.
King's Cross 27/10/46.
Neasden 20/8/47.
King's Cross 3/6/48.
Parkeston 19/8/51.
King's Cross 28/10/56.
Hitchin 23/6/57.
Hornsey 27/7/58.
Grantham 14/6/59.

RENUMBERED:
9561 31/3/46.
69561 23/2/50.

CONDEMNED: 24/5/61.
Into Don. for cut up 24/5/61.

892

Doncaster 1622.

To traffic 9/11/25.

REPAIRS:
Cow. ?/2—?/3/28.**G.**
Cow. ?—?/8/29.**L.**
Cow. ?/3—?/4/31.**G.**
Cow. ?/8—?/9/32.**L.**
Cow. ?/?—28/9/34.**G.**
Cow. ?/?—?/11/34.**L.**
Cow. ?/?—2/11/35.**H.**
Cow. ?/?—5/6/36.**G.**
Cow. ?/?—19/4/37.**L.**
Cow. 11—31/12/37.**G.**
Cow. ?/?—28/9/40.**G.**
Cow. 27/3—24/4/43.**G.**
Cow. ?/?—19/1/46.**L.**
Cow. 8/12/47—24/1/48.**G.**
Cow. ?/?—?/10/49.**C/L.**
Cow. 30/1—28/2/51.**H/I.**
Westinghouse brake replaced by steam.
Cow. 17/10—27/11/52.**G.**

BOILERS:
1380.
1382 *(ex894)* 2/11/35.
7585 *(ex4731)* 31/12/37.
1380 *(ex893)* 24/4/43.
1380 reno.21540 28/2/51.
21546 *(ex69553)* 27/11/52.

SHEDS:
Parkhead.
Kipps ?/9/38.
Parkhead ?/10/38.

RENUMBERED:
9562 19/5/46.

Engines which worked in Scotland had holders on the front plate of the smokebox to take their curved destination boards.

(right) Engines which moved south from their original Scottish allocation could be seen with both types of destination board holders. Doncaster works, 28th July 1957.

London District engines were fitted with tall lamp irons suitable for discs and also had an extra iron to carry two discs, or lamps, one above the other. This was for working goods trains to Southern Railway yards on which N2 were rarely, if ever, used.

Although the need for these extra irons ceased from 1923, they were still put on N2's built in 1928. Those with condensing gear got the tall iron, but even those for the Scottish Area had the five irons above buffer beam. King's Cross station.

In general, these redundant irons were removed at works visits from 1930, but only haphazardly.

(below) Not all the tall double irons were removed. London District No.69502 still had one when cut up in June 1958 and Scottish No.69503 was still carrying one at 3rd January 1957 withdrawal as shown on page 95, top. Doncaster works, 15th June 1958.

892 cont./
69562 28/2/51.

CONDEMNED: 12/1/56.
Cut up at Cowlairs 10/56.

893

Doncaster 1623.

To traffic 23/11/25.

REPAIRS:

Cow. ?/11—?/12/29.**G.**
(Cowlairs records missing).
Cow. ?—?/4/32.**H.**
Ghd. 29/6—1/7/32.**N/C.**
Raven fog signalling apparatus fitted.
Ghd. 26/9—13/10/32.**L.**
Cow. ?/?—10/5/34.**G.**
Cow. ?/?—?/1/35.**L.**
Cow. ?/?—3/10/36.**G.**
Cow. ?/?—9/12/36.**N/C.**
Cow. ?/?—?/1/37.**L.**
Cow. ?/?—18/11/39.**G.**
Cow. ?/?—4/2/42.**L.**
Cow. 20/6—25/7/42.**G.**
Cow. ?/?—19/12/42.**L.**
Cow. ?/?—12/6/44.**L.**
Cow. 27/10—24/11/45.**G.**
Cow. 14/5—12/6/48.**G.**
Tallowed down for storage 13/11/49.
Cow. 1—27/8/55.**G.**
Cow. 2—3/9/55.**N/C.**
Westinghouse brake replaced by steam.
Cow. 25/10—5/11/55.**C/L.**
Cow. 9—11/2/56.**C/L.**
Cow. 16—25/2/56.**N/C.**
Cow. 17—20/10/56.**N/C.**
Cow. 7/1—13/2/58.**H/I.**
Cow. 11—14/8/58.**N/C.**

BOILERS:
1381.
1380 *(ex892)* 3/10/36.
C1677 *(ex894)* 25/7/42.
1381 *(ex895)* 24/11/45.
1365 *(ex9553)* 12/6/48.
21538 *(ex69518)* 27/8/55.

SHEDS:
Parkhead.
Gateshead 21/4/32.
Kipps 12/11/32.
St Margarets 1/10/50.
Kipps 29/10/50.
Parkhead 22/12/52.

RENUMBERED:
9563 19/5/46.

69563 12/6/48.

CONDEMNED: 22/4/60.
Cut up at Cowlairs 28/5/60.

894

Doncaster 1625.

To traffic 25/11/25.

REPAIRS:
(Cowlairs records missing).
Cow.?/? —12/7/30.**?.**
(Cowlairs records missing).
Cow. ?/?—7/5/34.**G.**
Cow. ?/?—5/10/35.**G.**
Cow. ?/?—5/5/37.**G.**
Cow. ?/?—23/6/38.**L.**
Made fit to travel to Doncaster.
Don. ?/?—28/7/38.**G.**
Cow. ?/4—27/5/39.**L.**
Flaman speed recorder fitted.
Cow. 27/7—31/8/40.**G.**
Cow. ?/?—15/3/41.*Special.*
Cow. ?/?—26/6/43.**G.**
Cow. 17/11—8/12/45.**L.**
Cow. ?/?—1/5/46.**N/C.**
Cow. 19/8—6/9/47.**G.**
Cow. 21/12/49—12/1/50.**L/I.**
Westinghouse brake replaced by steam.
Cow. 25/9—6/11/54.**G.**
Cow. 5/11—1/12/56.**H/I.**
Cow. 4—5/12/56.**N/C.**
Not in use 105 days in 1944.

BOILERS:
1382.
C1677 *(ex4735)* 5/10/35.
C1707 *(ex2689)* 31/8/40.
8109 *(ex9596)* 6/9/47.
21550 *(exD1 62214)* 6/11/54.

SHEDS:
St Margarets.
Parkhead 4/6/32.
Carlisle Canal 26/8/57.

RENUMBERED:
9564 19/5/46.
69564 12/1/50.

CONDEMNED: 20/6/61.
Cut up at Cowlairs 2/10/62.

895

Doncaster 1628.

To traffic 9/12/25.

REPAIRS:
(Cowlairs records missing).
Cow. ?/9—?/10/30.**G.**
(Cowlairs records missing).
Cow. 24/6—15/7/33.**G.**
Cow. ?/?—21/2/35.**G.**
Cow. ?/?—18/4/36.**L.**
Cow. 6/3—14/4/37.**G.**
Cow. ?/?—26/11/38.**G.**
Cow. ?/?—26/10/40.**G.**
Cow. 23/10—20/11/43.**G.**
Cow. 14/5—15/6/46.**G.**
Cow. 14—18/5/48.**L.**
Cow. 23/5—18/6/49.**G.**
Westinghouse brake replaced by steam.
Cow. 6—8/10/49.**N/C.**
Cow. 21/6—14/7/50.**N/C.**
Cow. 11/9—6/10/51.**H/I.**
Cow. 5—31/10/53.**G.**
Cow. 22—31/12/53.**C/L.**
Cow. 15/3—2/4/55.**L/I.**
Cow. 6—10/3/56.**C/L.**
Cow. 20—24/8/57.**C/L.**
Cow. 26—28/9/57.**N/C.**

BOILERS:
1383.
1365 *(ex2586)* 15/7/33.
1381 *(ex893)* 14/4/37.
7585 *(ex892)* 20/11/43.
C1670 *(ex9595)* 18/6/49.
C1670 reno.21532 6/10/51.
21534 *(ex69507)* 31/10/53.

SHED:
Parkhead.

RENUMBERED:
9565 5/5/46.
69565 26/6/48.

CONDEMNED: 17/4/58.
Cut up at Kilmarnock 6/58.

896

Doncaster 1629.

To traffic 11/12/25.

REPAIRS:
Cow. 20—29/1/26.**N/C.**
Cow. 7—18/4/27.**L.**
Cow. 16/3—8/5/28.**G.**
Cow. 20—21/6/28.**N/C.**
Cow. 23/1—23/2/29.**G.**
Cow. 17/12/29—11/1/30.**L.**
Cow. 23/12/30—7/2/31.**G.**
Cow. 8/12/31—26/1/32.**G.**
Dar. 5—8/2/32.**N/C.**
Dar. 15/2—23/3/32.**N/C.**
Str. 22/8—1/10/35.**G.**
Str. 16/10—19/11/37.**G.**

Str. 10/3—5/4/38.**L.**
Westinghouse brake removed.
Don. 8/7—23/9/39.**G.**
Don. 23/2—19/4/42.**G.**
Don. 11/2—17/3/45.**G.**
Don. 11/10—26/11/47.**G.**
Don. 28/1—23/2/51.**G.**
Str. 30/11/53—30/1/54.**G.**

BOILERS:
1384.
8105 1/10/35.
1384 19/11/37.
9057 17/3/45.
21240 23/2/51.
21453 30/1/54.

SHEDS:
Kipps.
Stratford 30/1/32.
Hatfield 5/4/38.
Doncaster 2/5/42.
Mexborough 9/5/42.
King's Cross 16/3/46.
Hornsey 3/6/47.
Parkeston 19/8/51.
King's Cross 28/10/56.

RENUMBERED:
9566 27/7/46.
69566 23/2/51.

CONDEMNED: 17/6/57.
Into Don. for cut up 17/6/57.

897

Doncaster 1632.

To traffic 24/12/25.

REPAIRS:
Cow. 19—29/3/26.**N/C.**
Cow. 1/2—15/3/28.**G.**
Cow. 10/10—28/11/30.**G.**
Cow. 1/6—5/7/32.**G.**
Cow. 6—11/7/32.**N/C.**
Str. 14/2—13/4/34.**G.**
Str. 2/11/34—18/1/35.**G.**
Str. 10/12/35—11/1/36.**H.**
Str. 28/10—9/12/36.**G.**
Str. 10/10—2/12/38.**G.**
Westinghouse brake removed.
Don. 31/7—18/9/40.**G.**
Don. 4/2—22/3/43.**G.**
Don. 22/12/45—9/2/46.**G.**
Don. 25/3—28/4/47.**G.**
Don. 31/5—7/7/48.**G.**
Don. 25/4—25/5/51.**G.**
Str. 7/3—14/5/55.**G.**

BOILERS:
1385.
1384 11/1/36.

897 cont./
8098 9/12/36.
8100 2/12/38.
9617 28/4/47.
21276 25/5/51.
21369 14/5/55.

SHEDS:
Eastfield.
Parkhead 19/12/28.
Stratford 12/7/32.
Hatfield 2/12/38.
Doncaster 29/10/42.
Mexborough 17/10/43.
Neasden 17/11/43.
King's Cross 27/10/46.
Neasden 12/5/47.
King's Cross 6/6/48.
Hornsey 27/8/48.
Lincoln 27/10/48.
Hornsey 27/2/49.
King's Cross 9/9/51.
Hornsey 29/3/53.

RENUMBERED:
9567 28/7/46.
69567 7/7/48.

CONDEMNED: 28/4/59.
Into Don. for cut up 28/4/59.

2662

Hawthorn Leslie 3691.

To traffic 26/9/28.

REPAIRS:
Don. 14/3—23/4/30.**G.**
Don. 26/9—30/11/31.**G.**
Don. 23/6—31/8/33.**G.**
Don. 19/4—21/5/35.**G.**
Don. 7/3—20/5/37.**G.**
Str. 10/5—27/6/39.**G.**
Str. 22/8—21/10/42.**G.**
Don. 31/8—1/10/43.**L.**
Don. 13/3—5/5/45.**G.**
Don. 11/1—4/2/46.**L.**
Don. 3/3—9/4/48.**G.**
Don. 6/8—15/10/48.**L.**
Don. 19/11—20/12/50.**G.**
Str. 19/1—27/2/54.**G.**
Str. 19/9—26/10/55.**C/L.**
Don. 19/7—25/8/56.**G.**
Don. 14/4—22/5/59.**G.**

BOILERS:
8090.
7594 21/5/35.
1373 20/5/37.
8108 27/6/39.
8538 5/5/45.
21409 *(new)* 20/12/50.
21305 27/2/54.

21238 25/8/56.
21425 22/5/59.

SHEDS:
Ardsley.
King's Cross 13/10/28.
Hornsey 6/10/57.
King's Cross 24/11/57.
New England 20/5/62.

RENUMBERED:
9568 14/4/46.
69568 9/4/48.

CONDEMNED: 16/9/62.
Into Don. for cut up 12/3/63.

2663

Hawthorn Leslie 3692.

To traffic 1/10/28.

REPAIRS:
Don. 26—30/10/28.**L.**
Don. 15/3—3/5/30.**G.**
Don. 24/10/31—4/1/32.**G.**
Don. 19/9—14/11/33.**G.**
Don. 16/2—21/3/36.**G.**
Don. 8/1—24/2/38.**G.**
Don. 8/12/39—13/1/40.**G.**
Str. 27/11/42—16/2/43.**G.**
Don. 31/1—14/3/45.**G.**
Don. 20/8—3/11/47.**G.**
Don. 3—19/12/48.**L.**
Don. 2—6/1/49.**N/C.**
Don. 1/10—3/11/50.**G.**
Don. 18/5—12/6/53.**G.**
Str. 13/5—24/7/54.**C/L.**
Str. 4—6/8/54.**N/C.**
Don. 11/1—11/2/56.**G.**
Don. 20/3/59. *Not repaired.*

BOILERS:
8091.
8139 21/3/36.
8105 24/2/38.
8097 16/2/43.
8542 14/3/45.
21401 *(new)* 3/11/50.
21463 12/6/53.

SHEDS:
Ardsley.
King's Cross 9/11/28.

RENUMBERED:
9569 14/4/46.
69569 19/12/48.

CONDEMNED: 23/3/59.
Cut up at Doncaster.

2664

Hawthorn Leslie 3693.

To traffic 5/10/28.

REPAIRS:
Don. 24—27/10/28.**L.**
Don. 1/4—8/5/30.**G.**
Don. 24/10—7/1/32.**G.**
Don. 10/11/33—13/1/34.**G.**
Don. 24/8—17/10/35.**G.**
Don. 2/9—5/10/37.**G.**
Don. 28/10—19/12/39.**G.**
Str. 15/10—21/12/42.**G.**
Don. 22/2—30/3/46.**G.**
Don. 16/9—26/10/48.**G.**
Don. 15/6—17/7/51.**G.**
Don. 15/12/53—16/1/54.**G.**
Don. 22/2—1/3/54.**N/C.**
Don. 14/1—13/2/57.**G.**
Don. 15—19/2/57.**N/C.**

BOILERS:
8092.
8097 5/10/37.
9327 21/12/42.
9139 26/10/48.
21288 17/7/51.
21236 16/1/54.
21409 13/2/57.

SHEDS:
Ardsley.
King's Cross 22/11/28.

RENUMBERED:
9570 30/3/46.
69570 23/10/48.

CONDEMNED: 15/12/59.
Into Don. for cut up 15/12/59.

2665

Hawthorn Leslie 3694.

To traffic 19/10/28.

REPAIRS:
Don. 7—10/11/28.**L.**
Don. 19/4—5/6/30.**G.**
Don. 18/9—30/10/31.**G.**
Don. 26/8—16/10/33.**G.**
Don. 23/1—21/2/36.**G.**
Str. 6/11—7/12/37.**G.**
Don. 7/8—6/10/39.**G.**
Str. 11/1—2/5/43.**G.**
Don. 14/4—15/6/46.**G.**
Don. 7/10—27/11/48.**G.**
Don. 24/5—15/6/51.**G.**
Don. 17/1—12/3/53.**C/H.**
Str. 10/10—13/11/54.**G.**
Str. 2/8—12/10/57.**G.**

BOILERS:
8093.
1370 21/2/36.
7574 7/12/37.
8133 2/5/43.
9327 27/11/48.
21282 15/6/51.
21365 13/11/54.
21302 12/10/57.

SHEDS:
Ardsley.
King's Cross 20/11/28.
Hatfield 5/4/59.
New England 14/6/59.

RENUMBERED:
9571 14/4/46.
69571 27/11/48.

CONDEMNED: 1/6/61.
Into Don. for cut up 1/6/61.

2666

Hawthorn Leslie 3695.

To traffic 23/10/28.

REPAIRS:
Don. 15—19/11/28.**L.**
Don. 2/4—16/5/30.**G.**
Don. 1/8—2/10/31.**G.**
Don. 23/6—16/8/33.**G.**
Don. 9/1—9/2/35.**G.**
Str. 20/8—2/10/36.**G.**
Str. 28/9—17/11/38.**G.**
Don. 22/2—12/4/41.**G.**
Don. 22/3—21/4/44.**G.**
Str. 5/12/46—30/3/47.**G.**
Don. 17/7—26/8/49.**G.**
Don. 2—30/5/52.**G.**
Str. 6/9—9/10/54.**G.**
Str. 11/11/54—22/1/55.**C/L.**
Str. 15/8—14/9/55.**N/C.**
Str. 23/2—29/3/58.**G.**

BOILERS:
8094.
1367 9/2/35.
1385 2/10/36.
8281 17/11/38.
9178 26/8/49.
21414 *(new)* 30/5/52.
21311 9/10/54.
21362 29/3/58.

SHEDS:
Ardsley.
King's Cross 6/12/28.
Hornsey 29/9/57.
King's Cross 15/11/59.

(above) **No.2689 was moved from Scotland to work from Gateshead in the NE Area on 25th December 1931. It was followed there by No.2690 (5th February 1932) and 893 (21st April 1933) and they were fitted with Raven fog signalling apparatus. This was removed when they returned to Scottish sheds from November 1932 to June 1933.**

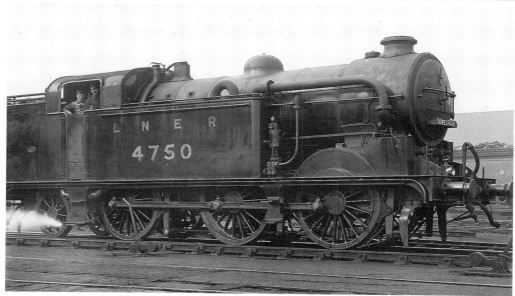

(right) **With the exception of Nos.892 to 897, all originally had only vacuum brake, on the engine and for train working.**

To be useful in the Glasgow area, Nos.892 to 897 were fitted with Westinghouse pump for engine and train brakes and also had vacuum for train working. The pumps were fixed onto the front end of the tank on the driver's side; left-hand in the case of Nos.892 to 897 and right side for the 4721 series (*see* next).

(*left*) **When Nos.4721 to 4740 went to Scotland in 1927/8, Cowlairs added Westinghouse for train braking to twelve:- Nos.4721 to 4724, 4726, 4728, 4729, 4731, 4732, 4735, 4737 and 4740. Eastfield shed, May 1928.**

(*below*) **By 1932 Nos.896, 897, 4722, 4723, 4726, 4737 and 4740 had been transferred to the GE Section of Southern Area and from April 1938 to March 1940 the Westinghouse brake was taken off. For Nos.896 and 897 the engine brake was then converted to vacuum.**

Beginning with No.4732, ex-Cowlairs 1st November 1945, Westinghouse was gradually removed from the eleven Scottish engines so fitted (*see* 69564 on page 66, bottom left), and Nos.9562 to 9565 were then converted to steam brake on the engine. It was not until ex-Cowlairs 3rd September 1955 that 69563 was changed. Parkhead shed, May 1953.

2666 cont./
RENUMBERED:
9572 14/4/46.
69572 26/8/49.

CONDEMNED: 11/3/61.
Into Don. for cut up 11/3/61.

2667

Hawthorn Leslie 3696.

To traffic 3/11/28.

REPAIRS:
Don. 5—9/11/28.**L.**
Don. 3/5—28/6/30.**G.**
Don. 5/12/31—22/2/32.**G.**
Don. 8/12/33—9/2/34.**G.**
Don. 16/8—24/9/35.**G.**
Don. 30/4—26/6/37.**G.**
Str. 29/12/38—18/2/39.**G.**
Don. 25/5—1/7/41.**G.**
Don. 22/11—18/12/43.**G.**
Don. 11/5—19/6/47.**G.**
Don. ?/?—27/7/47.**N/C.**
Don. 7/6—12/7/50.**G.**
Don. 21/1—13/2/53.**G.**
Str. 21/11/55—14/1/56.**G.**
Don. 31/12/57—30/1/58.**C/L.**
Don. 21/11/58. *Not repaired.*

BOILERS:
8095.
8090 26/6/37.
8099 18/2/39.
8939 12/7/50.
21233 13/2/53.
21404 14/1/56.

SHEDS:
Ardsley.
King's Cross 26/11/28.

RENUMBERED:
9573 14/4/46.
69573 12/7/50.

CONDEMNED: 24/11/58.
Cut up at Doncaster.

2668

Hawthorn Leslie 3697.

To traffic 9/11/28.

REPAIRS:
Don. 21—24/11/28.**L.**
Don. 2/7—30/9/30.**G.**
Don. 9/4—8/8/32.**G.**
Don. 26/1—24/3/34.**G.**
Don. 28/2—11/4/36.**G.**

Str. 4/2—17/3/38.**G.**
Don. 24/4—1/6/40.**G.**
Don. 22/11—18/12/43.**G.**
Don. 23/10—7/12/46.**G.**
Don. 11/6—19/7/49.**G.**
Don. 3/11—1/12/49.**C/L.**
Don. 29/5—7/7/52.**G.**
Str. 21/7—26/8/54.**G.**
Str. 16—20/9/54.**N/C.**
Str. 27—30/9/54.**N/C.**
Str. 12/10—22/11/57.**G.**
Str. 10—28/2/58.**N/C.**

BOILERS:
8096.
7590 11/4/36.
8133 17/3/38.
8997 1/6/40.
9069 7/12/46.
21365 7/7/52.
21340 26/8/54.
21309 22/11/57.

SHEDS:
Ardsley.
King's Cross 10/12/28.

RENUMBERED:
9574 27/7/46.
69574 19/7/49.

CONDEMNED: 14/2/61.
Into Don. for cut up 14/2/61.

2669

Hawthorn Leslie 3698.

To traffic 20/11/28.

REPAIRS:
Don. 23—28/11/28.**L.**
Don. 16/12/29—8/2/30.**G.**
Don. 25/7—18/9/31.**G.**
Don. 15/12/31—2/3/32.**L.**
Don. 9/9—27/10/33.**G.**
*Special vacuum ejector to
Drawing J381N.*
Don. 14/6—24/7/35.**G.**
Don. 22/4—12/6/37.**G.**
Str. 25/4—17/6/39.**G.**
Str. 8/5—2/8/42.**G.**
Don. 22/7—31/8/45.**G.**
Don. 2/4—10/5/48.**G.**
Don. 23/4—26/5/50.**G.**
Don. 27/10—21/11/52.**G.**
Str. 27/4—30/5/53.**N/C.**
Str. 3/10—19/11/55.**G.**
Str. 5/4—16/6/56.**C/L.**
Don. 13/11—18/12/58.**G.**
Don. 23/3—7/4/59.**C/L.**

BOILERS:
8097.

8108 12/6/37.
8090 17/6/39.
8986 10/5/48.
8993 26/5/50.
21387 21/11/52.
21208 19/11/55.
21327 18/12/58.

SHEDS:
Ardsley.
King's Cross 26/12/28.
New England 10/9/61.

RENUMBERED:
9575 27/7/46.
69575 8/5/48.

CONDEMNED: 16/9/62.
Into Don. for cut up 19/2/63.

2670

Hawthorn Leslie 3699.

To traffic 28/11/28.

REPAIRS:
Don. 30/11—4/12/28.**L.**
Don. 26/10/30—6/1/31.**G.**
Don. 27/8—1/11/32.**G.**
Don. 9—12/11/32.**L.**
After collision.
Don. 29/9/33—21/4/34.**G.**
Don. 25/3—30/4/36.**G.**
Don. 26/5—15/6/37.**L.**
Str. 19/6—29/7/38.**G.**
T.A.B. valves fitted.
Don. 2/9—9/10/40.**G.**
Don. 16/10—2/12/43.**G.**
Don. 9—29/3/44.**G.**
Don. 16/2—11/4/47.**G.**
Don. 30/1—7/3/49.**G.**
Don. 18/11/50—3/1/51.**G.**
Don. 22—31/151.**N/C.**
Don. 22/3—4/4/51.**C/L.**
Don. 22/9—23/10/53.**G.**
Str. 20/2—7/4/56.**G.**

BOILERS:
8098.
8099 30/4/36.
8103 29/7/38.
9056 11/4/47.
21230 3/1/51.
21256 23/10/53.
21392 7/4/56.

SHEDS:
Ardsley.
King's Cross 28/12/28.

RENUMBERED:
9576 27/7/46.
69576 7/3/49.

CONDEMNED: 22/7/59.
Into Don. for cut up 22/7/59.

2671

Hawthorn Leslie 3700.

To traffic 4/12/28.

REPAIRS:
Don. 7—11/12/28.**L.**
Don. 26/5—31/7/30.**G.**
Don. 16/1—31/3/32.**G.**
Don. 3/2—1/5/34.**G.**
Don. 6/3—21/4/46.**G.**
Don. 28/3—4/5/38.**G.**
Don. 20/6—13/7/40.**G.**
Don. 6/8—11/9/40.**L.**
Don. 23/7—28/8/43.**G.**
Don. 20/7—24/8/46.**G.**
Don. 10/12/48—12/1/49.**G.**
Don. 16/8—19/9/51.**G.**
Str. 14/12/53—13/3/54.**G.**
Don. 16/8—6/10/56.**G.**

BOILERS:
8099.
8091 21/4/36.
7590 4/5/38.
9331 28/8/43.
8106 24/8/46.
10521 12/1/49.
21305 19/9/51.
21295 13/3/54.
21264 6/10/56.

SHEDS:
Ardsley.
King's Cross 27/12/28.
Hatfield 1/2/59.

RENUMBERED:
9577 24/8/46.
69577 12/1/49.

CONDEMNED: 5/5/59.
Into Don. for cut up 5/5/59.

2672

Hawthorn Leslie 3701.

To traffic 8/1/29.

REPAIRS:
Don. 10—23/1/29.**L.**
Don. 19/10—13/12/30.**G.**
Don. 14/5—31/8/32.**G.**
Don. 14/9—18/10/34.**G.**
Don. 25/7—28/8/36.**G.**
Str. 6/8—22/9/38.**G.**
Don. 28/10—28/11/40.**G.**
Don. 10/9—23/10/43.**G.**

(*left*) The Westinghouse brake did finally disappear from N2 class and 69563 ran from 3rd September 1955 to 22nd April 1960 with steam brake on engine and vacuum for train. Parkhead shed, March 1959.

(*below*) From July 1925 engines to Metropolitan gauge were fitted with trip cock, the off-side trip being just in front of the radial wheel. Doncaster shed.

(left) In 1947 London Transport stipulated that the trip cock must be within 5 feet of the leading axle, so that on the right hand side had to be moved to a position ahead of the front footstep. Neasden shed, August 1947.

(below) On the left hand side, the trip cock did not need to be moved, because it already met the stipulation when the engine ran with bunker leading.

2672 cont./
Don. 11/7—24/8/46.**G.**
Don. 23/1—22/2/47.**G.**
Don. 20/11/48—3/1/49.**G.**
Don. 26/4—25/5/51.**G.**
Don. 25/11—23/12/53.**G.**
Don. 26/9—27/10/56.**G.**
Don. 31/10—1/11/56.**N/C.**

BOILERS:
8100.
8109 22/9/38.
1370 28/11/40.
8285 24/8/46.
21275 25/5/51.
21272 23/12/53.
21401 27/10/56.

SHEDS:
Ardsley.
King's Cross 8/2/29.

RENUMBERED:
9578 24/8/46.
69578 3/1/49.

CONDEMNED: 25/11/59.
Into Don. for cut up 25/11/59.

_____

2673

Hawthorn Leslie 3702.

To traffic 11/1/29.

REPAIRS:
Don. 17/1—8/2/29.**L.**
Don. 13/12/30—4/3/31.**G.**
Don. 27/8—24/10/32.**G.**
Don. 23/2—19/5/34.**G.**
Don. 4/4—20/5/36.**G.**
Don. 13/2—26/3/38.**G.**
Don. 21/1—26/2/40.**G.**
Don. 24/6—7/8/43.**G.**
Don. 21/2—20/3/44.**H.**
Don. 30/9—14/11/45.**G.**
Don. 8/3—19/4/48.**G.**
Don. 14/10—9/11/50.**G.**
Don. 14—30/1/52.**C/L.**
Don. 20/4—13/5/53.**G.**
Str. 4/1—25/2/56.**G.**
Str. 26/3—26/4/56.**N/C.**
Don. 18/9—6/11/58.**G.**

BOILERS:
8101.
8093 20/5/36.
8834 19/4/48.
21222 9/11/50.
21461 13/5/53.
21233 25/2/56.
21293 6/11/58.

SHEDS:
Ardsley.
King's Cross 5/3/29.
Hornsey 17/7/60.
New England 9/7/61.

RENUMBERED:
9579 10/8/46.
69579 19/4/48.

CONDEMNED: 16/9/62.
Into Don. for cut up 31/10/62.

_____

2674

Hawthorn Leslie 3703.

To traffic 15/1/29.

REPAIRS:
Don. 4/2—5/3/29.**L.**
Don. 15/9—7/11/30.**G.**
Don. 21/5—25/8/32.**G.**
Gor. 2/6—4/8/34.**G.**
Don. 29/3—2/5/36.**G.**
Str. 8/3—22/4/38.**G.**
Don. 14/5—13/6/40.**G.**
Str. 4/6—5/8/42.**H/I.**
Don. 16/4—18/5/44.**G.**
Don. 9/10—9/11/46.**G.**
Don. 1/6—21/7/48.**G.**
Don. 19/9—18/10/50.**G.**
Don. 26/3—24/4/53.**G.**
Str. 7/11—15/12/55.**G.**
Str. 13—19/1/56.**N/C.**
Don. 7/7—11/8/58.**G.**

BOILERS:
8102.
8107 22/4/38.
8095 18/5/44.
8804 21/7/48.
21215 18/10/50.
21459 24/4/53.
21350 15/12/55.
21336 11/8/58.

SHEDS:
Ardsley.
King's Cross 21/3/29.
Hornsey 21/9/32.
King's Cross 7/11/32.
Hatfield 11/2/45.
King's Cross 15/11/53.
Hatfield 3/1/54.
King's Cross 20/6/54.
Hatfield 5/9/54.
King's Cross 16/3/58.
Hatfield 26/7/59.
Grantham 12/6/60.
New England 21/5/61.

RENUMBERED:
9580 14/4/46.

69580 17/7/48.

CONDEMNED: 11/9/61.
Into Don. for cut up 11/9/61.

_____

2675

Hawthorn Leslie 3704.

To traffic 29/1/29.

REPAIRS:
Don. 25/2—1/3/29.**L.**
Don. 3/10—26/11/30.**G.**
Don. 23/7—8/10/32.**G.**
Don. 9/3—12/5/34.**G.**
Don. 19/6—17/7/36.**G.**
Don. 29/3—7/5/38.**G.**
Str. 13/7—6/8/38.**L.**
Don. 23/5—21/6/40.**G.**
Don. 27/8—3/10/43.**G.**
Don. 9/10—25/11/44.**G.**
Don. 28/12/46—11/3/47.**G.**
Don. 20/2—30/3/48.**G.**
Don. 28/2—28/3/51.**G.**
Don. 12/8—18/9/53.**G.**
Str. 18/3—2/4/54.**C/L.**
Don. 25/4—31/5/56.**G.**
Don. 2—5/6/56.**N/C.**
Don. 12/1—13/2/59.**G.**

BOILERS:
8103.
9066 7/5/38.
8806 30/3/48.
21256 28/3/51.
21223 18/9/53.
21425 *(new)* 31/5/56.
21421 13/2/59.

SHEDS:
Ardsley.
King's Cross 20/3/29.
Hatfield 20/2/35.
King's Cross 24/4/35.

RENUMBERED:
9581 20/7/46.
69581 27/3/48.

CONDEMNED: 1/12/60.
Into Don. for cut up 1/12/60.

_____

2676

Hawthorn Leslie 3705.

To traffic 1/2/29.

REPAIRS:
Don. 7—12/3/29.**L.**
Don. 2/11/30—15/1/31.**G.**
Don. 23/7—13/10/32.**G.**

Gor. 27/4—14/7/34.**G.**
Don. 20/7—19/8/36.**G.**
Str. 11/4—28/5/38.**G.**
T.A.B. valves fitted.
Str. 25/2—6/5/39.**G.**
Don. 21/12/41—20/2/42.**G.**
Don. 2—30/3/44.**G.**
Don. 8/7—17/8/46.**G.**
Don. 24/4—31/5/48.**G.**
Don. 27/9—25/10/50.**G.**
Don. 23/7—22/8/52.**G.**
Str. 6/12/54—15/1/55.**G.**
Str. 13/10—14/12/57.**G.**
Don. 19/9/60. *Not repaired.*

BOILERS:
8104.
7552 28/5/38.
8106 20/2/42.
9620 17/8/46.
21217 25/10/50.
21419 *(new)* 22/8/52.
21291 15/1/55.
21253 14/12/57.

SHEDS:
Ardsley.
King's Cross 26/3/29.
Hatfield 10/8/34.
New England 14/6/59.

RENUMBERED:
9582 14/4/46.
69582 29/5/48.

CONDEMNED: 26/9/60.
Cut up at Doncaster.

_____

2677

Hawthorn Leslie 3706.

To traffic 15/2/29.

REPAIRS:
Don. 13—23/3/29.**L.**
Don. 26/9—17/11/30.**G.**
Don. 25/6—22/9/32.**G.**
Gor. 14/7—15/9/34.**G.**
Don. 30/7—25/8/36.**G.**
Str. 31/7—13/9/38.**G.**
Don. 16/1—22/2/41.**G.**
Don. 26/3—22/4/44.**G.**
Don. 3/11—28/12/46.**G.**
Don. 23/10—27/11/47.**L.**
Don. 15/11—19/12/49.**G.**
Don. 5—29/8/52.**G.**
Str. 22/11—24/12/54.**G.**
Str. 20/2—2/5/58.**G.**

BOILERS:
8105.
8281 15/9/34.
8137 13/9/38.

The Scottish based engines continued to carry GNR type brackets for the destination boards on the back of the bunker and were not fitted with the North British Railway variety. Note the toe hole cut above cab footstep. Kittybrewster shed.

This amenity was not applied until quite late on some, No.69511 being still without it to at least July 1952, although the illustration in the centre of page 109, shows it was put in. Note transposition of blower and ejector exhaust compared with No.69503. Kipps shed, July 1951.

All the first sixty had fully lined green livery when new and at Grouping.

No.1606 was the first to be repainted - in black and with single red lining. The number was moved to tank and applied in 12in. shaded transfers. From 29th September 1923 (1606) to 2nd February 1924 (1726) area suffix N was added. Those to get it were Nos.1606, 1721 to 1724, 1726, 1729, 1749, 1761, 1763 and 1767.

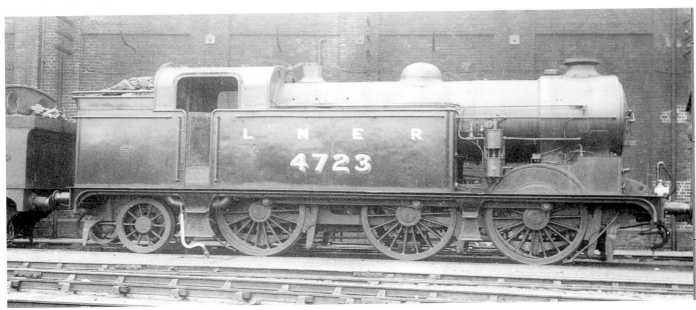

(above) Beginning with No.4731, ex-works 26th January 1924, all then got LNER number and until November 1941 had red lining applied. Stratford works, June 1935.

(left) From July 1942 until January 1946 only NE was used, but in 12in. figures instead of the 7$\frac{1}{2}$in. for LNER. Nottingham Victoria, May 1946.

CLASS N 2

2677 cont./
1364 22/2/41.
9623 28/12/46.
8534 19/12/49.
21372 29/8/52.
21319 24/12/54.
21259 2/5/58.

SHEDS:
Ardsley.
King's Cross 8/4/29.
Grantham 12/2/61.
New England 21/5/61.

RENUMBERED:
9583 20/7/46.
69583 17/12/49.

CONDEMNED: 16/9/62.
Into Don. for cut up 13/2/63.

2678

Hawthorn Leslie 3707.

To traffic 22/2/29.

REPAIRS:
Don. 18—26/3/29.**L.**
Don. 14/12/30—6/3/31.**G.**
Don. 17/9—8/11/32.**G.**
Gor. 22/3—30/6/34.**G.**
Don. 2—31/7/36.**G.**
Str. 27/5—4/7/38.**G.**
T.A.B. valves fitted.
Don. 4/7—2/8/40.**G.**
Don. 24/10—22/11/43.**G.**
Don. 8/5—6/7/46.**G.**
Don. 24/10—10/12/48.**G.**
Don. 11—28/4/50.**C/L.**
Don. 8/7—18/8/50.**C/L.**
Don. 10/7—3/8/51.**G.**
Str. 13—20/2/52.**N/C.**
Str. 4/5—24/7/54.**G.**
Str. 5/9—26/10/57.**G.**

BOILERS:
8106.
8102 4/7/38.
9614 6/7/46.
21291 3/8/51.
21309 24/7/54.
21365 26/10/57.

SHEDS:
Ardsley.
King's Cross 17/4/29.
Neasden 27/10/46.
King's Cross 21/10/47.

RENUMBERED:
9584 6/7/46.
69584 10/12/48.

CONDEMNED: 10/7/59.
Into Don. for cut up 10/7/59.

2679

Hawthorn Leslie 3708.

To traffic 6/3/29.

REPAIRS:
Don. 2—18/4/29.**L.**
Don. 28/11/30—18/2/31.**G.**
Don. 8/10—13/12/32.**G.**
Don. 26/2—26/4/34.**G.**
Don. 4/4—9/5/36.**G.**
Str. 29/1—5/3/38.**G.**
Don. 25/4—30/5/40.**G.**
Don. 17/2—22/3/41.**L.**
Don. 4/12/43—1/1/44.**G.**
Don. 2—29/8/44.**L.**
Don. 23/6—20/8/47.**G.**
Don. 9/5—2/6/50.**G.**
Don. 4—31/10/52.**G.**
Str. 29/4—24/6/55.**G.**
Don. 19/6—29/7/58.**G.**

BOILERS:
8107.
1370 5/3/38.
1367 30/5/40.
9329 1/1/44.
9262 2/6/50.
21382 31/10/52.
21372 24/6/55.
21311 29/7/58.

SHEDS:
Ardsley.
King's Cross 7/5/29.

RENUMBERED:
9585 20/7/46.
69585 2/6/50.

CONDEMNED: 23/9/61.
Into Don. for cut up 23/9/61.

2680

Hawthorn Leslie 3709.

To traffic 20/3/29.

REPAIRS:
Don. 25/4—8/5/29.**L.**
Don. 30/11—12/2/31.**G.**
Don. 12/11/32—30/1/33.**G.**
Don. 2/2—12/3/35.**G.**
Don. 11/2—19/3/37.**G.**
Str. 1/4—27/5/39.**G.**
Don. 24/9—6/11/43.**G.**
Don. 8/4—18/5/46.**G.**
Don. 5/7—4/8/48.**G.**

Don. 16/5—22/6/50.**G.**
Don. 27/3—25/4/52.**G.**
Str. 31/12/54—5/2/55.**G.**
Str. 16/1—8/3/58.**G.**
Don. 19—24/12/58.**N/C.**

BOILERS:
8108.
7681 19/3/37.
1369 27/5/39.
8937 18/5/46.
9791 22/6/50.
21412 *(new)* 25/4/52.
21370 5/2/55.
21419 8/3/58.

SHEDS:
Ardsley.
King's Cross 27/5/29.
Hornsey 24/3/33.
Hatfield 5/1/42.
King's Cross 31/5/53.
Hatfield 18/10/53.
King's Cross 20/3/60.

RENUMBERED:
9586 18/5/46.
69586 31/7/48.

CONDEMNED: 3/3/61.
Into Don. for cut up 3/3/61.

2681

Hawthorn Leslie 3710.

To traffic 10/4/29.

REPAIRS:
Don. 7—18/5/29.**L.**
Don. 17/1—23/3/31.**G.**
Don. 6/8—19/10/32.**G.**
Don. 17/8—27/9/34.**G.**
Don. 1—27/7/36.**G.**
Str. 19/6—2/8/38.**G.**
T.A.B. valves fitted.
Str. 1—6/10/38.**L.**
Str. 28/2—16/3/39.**L.**
Don. 2/4—3/5/41.**G.**
Str. 3/4—20/8/43.**G.**
Don. 14/11/45—31/1/46.**G.**
Don. 25/2—2/4/48.**G.**
Don. 18/7—14/8/50.**G.**
Don. 15/9—24/10/52.**G.**
Don. 13/5—14/6/56.**G.**
Don. 8/7/60. *Not repaired.*

BOILERS:
8109.
8106 2/8/38.
9264 3/5/41.
8285 20/8/43.
C1681 31/1/46.
9132 2/4/48.

8995 14/8/50.
21217 24/10/52.
21426 *(new)* 14/6/56.

SHEDS:
Ardsley.
King's Cross 30/5/29.
Hornsey 12/12/41.
Hatfield 4/1/42.
King's Cross 27/9/53.
Hornsey 3/1/54.

RENUMBERED:
9587 21/7/46.
69587 2/4/48.

CONDEMNED: 11/7/60.
Cut up at Doncaster.

2682

Yorkshire Engine Co. 2220.

To traffic 25/9/28.

REPAIRS:
Don. 21—25/8/28.**L.**
Don. 12/7—11/9/30.**G.**
Don. 7/5—20/8/32.**G.**
Nicolai piston valves fitted.
Don. 9/3—13/6/34.**G.**
Don. 28/2—7/4/36.**G.**
Nicolai piston valves removed.
Str. 30/1—11/3/38.**G.**
Don. 12/8—21/9/40.**G.**
Don. 8/1—12/2/44.**G.**
Don. 24/2—20/4/47.**G.**
Don. 19/11—23/12/49.**G.**
Don. 12/3—8/4/52.**G.**
Str. 19/7—23/9/55.**G.**
Don. 16/2—27/3/58.**G.**
Str. 15/2/60. *Not repaired.*

BOILERS:
8133.
8139 11/3/38.
1366 20/4/47.
9324 23/12/49.
21347 8/4/52.
21382 23/9/55.
21360 27/3/58.

SHEDS:
Doncaster.
King's Cross 16/10/28.
Hatfield 31/10/47.
King's Cross 31/5/53.
Hatfield 19/7/53.
King's Cross 24/1/54.
Hatfield 27/6/54.

RENUMBERED:
9588 10/8/46.
69588 23/12/49.

9588 cont./
CONDEMNED: 29/2/60.
Cut up at Stratford.

2683

Yorkshire Engine Co. 2221.

To traffic 6/10/28.

REPAIRS:
Don. 3—6/10/28.**L.**
Don. 18—20/10/28.**L.**
Don. 20/3—3/5/30.**G.**
Don. 10/10—5/12/31.**G.**
Don. 18/8—11/10/33.**G.**
Don. 24/5—29/6/35.**G.**
Don. 26/2—24/3/37.**G.**
Str. 19/3—6/5/39.**G.**
Don. 29/1—1/3/41.**L.**
Cracked buffer beam.
Don. 27/11/41—13/1/42.**G.**
Don. 21/1—1/3/45.**G.**
Str. 8/1—8/7/47.**G.**
Don. 13/5—20/6/49.**G.**
Don. 6—29/2/52.**G.**
Str. 10/5—12/6/54.**G.**
Don. 10/4—18/5/57.**G.**
Don. 22—24/5/57.**N/C.**
Don. 31/1—15/2/58.**N/C.**

BOILERS:
8134.
8090 29/6/35.
1369 24/3/37.
1385 6/5/39.
9324 13/1/42.
10527 20/6/49.
21340 29/2/52.
21329 12/6/54.
21414 18/5/57.

SHEDS:
Doncaster.
King's Cross 6/11/28.
Hatfield 19/4/29.
King's Cross 6/1/30.
Hornsey 28/9/41.
Hatfield 7/12/41.
King's Cross 14/12/41.

RENUMBERED:
9589 20/7/46.
69589 20/6/49.

CONDEMNED: 7/3/60.
Cut up at Stratford 7/3/60.

2684

Yorkshire Engine Co. 2222.

To traffic 2/11/28.

REPAIRS:
Don. 30/10—2/11/28.**L.**
Don. 1/4—14/5/30.**G.**
Don. 24/10/31—4/1/32.**L.**
Don. 27/10—9/12/33.**G.**
Don. 13/6—20/7/35.**G.**
Don. 7/3—24/4/37.**G.**
Str. 3/4—2/6/39.**G.**
Don. 9/2—9/4/42.**G.**
Don. 20/6—28/7/45.**G.**
Str. 11/11/46—11/1/47.**G.**
Don. 10/8—17/9/48.**G.**
Don. 18/9—17/10/51.**G.**
Str. 22/3—15/5/54.**G.**
Str. 7/12/55—14/1/56.**C/L.**

BOILERS:
8135.
7681 2/6/39.
9144 17/9/48.
21309 17/10/51.
21274 15/5/54.

SHEDS:
Doncaster.
King's Cross 20/12/28.
Doncaster 2/5/42.
Mexborough 9/5/42.
King's Cross 16/3/46.
Hatfield 25/5/47.
King's Cross 17/7/49.
Stratford 13/7/52.
Parkeston 27/7/52.
King's Cross 3/8/52.
Hornsey 19/10/52.
King's Cross 29/3/53.

RENUMBERED:
9590 10/8/46.
69590 17/9/48.

CONDEMNED: 3/6/57.
Into Don. for cut up 3/6/57.

2685

Yorkshire Engine Co. 2223.

To traffic 20/12/28.

REPAIRS:
Don. 30/11—5/12/28.**L.**
Cow. 21—24/12/28.**L.**
Cow. 28/5—2/7/31.**G.**

Don. 28/8—15/10/31.**L.**
Condensing and trip cock gear fitted.
Don. 6/7—20/9/33.**G.**
Don. 3/5—8/6/35.**G.**
Don. 24/4—26/5/37.**G.**
Str. 25/3—11/5/39.**G.**
Str. 26/4—24/6/42.**G.**
Don. 22/5—7/7/45.**G.**
Don. 20/8—8/9/45.**L.**
Superheater header flange.
Don. 10/2—12/3/48.**G.**
Don. 28/7—26/8/49.**C/L.**
Don. 30/3—27/4/51.**G.**
Don. 16/11—18/12/53.**G.**
Str. 22/4—1/6/54.**C/L.**
Str. 10/2—28/3/56.**C/L.**
Don. 26/10—24/11/56.**G.**

BOILERS:
8136.
8098 11/5/39.
9790 12/3/48.
21264 27/4/51.
21261 18/12/53.
21271 24/11/56.

SHEDS:
Doncaster.
Scotland 20/12/28.
Haymarket 26/12/28.
Doncaster 8/7/31.
King's Cross 15/10/31.
Hatfield 12/10/42.
Hornsey 19/12/43.
King's Cross 30/1/44.
Hatfield 1/2/59.

RENUMBERED:
9591 10/8/46.
ᴇ9591 12/3/48.
69591 26/8/49.

CONDEMNED: 5/8/59.
Into Don. for cut up 5/8/59.

2686

Yorkshire Engine Co. 2224.

To traffic 29/12/28.

REPAIRS:
Don. 6—11/12/28.**L.**
Cow. 31/12/28—7/1/29.**L.**
Cow. 17/10—18/11/30.**G.**
Don. 16/12/31—29/2/32.**G.**
Condensing and trip cock gear fitted.
Don. 16/12/33—23/2/34.**G.**

Don. 14/5—27/7/34.**L.**
Don. 19/6—18/7/36.**G.**
Str. 7/4—23/5/38.**G.**
Don. 20/1—6/4/39.**L.**
Don. 20/11/40—10/1/41.**G.**
Don. 8/1—10/2/44.**G.**
Don. 11/10—30/11/46.**G.**
Don. 5/6—15/7/49.**G.**
Don. 14/6—18/7/52.**G.**
Str. 25/10—27/11/54.**G.**
Str. 3—5/1/55.**N/C.**
Str. 2/1—21/2/58.**G.**
Don. 5—26/5/59.**C/H.**

BOILERS:
8137.
7566 23/5/38.
8094 10/2/44.
9622 30/11/46.
21367 18/7/52.
21336 27/11/54.
21351 21/2/58.

SHEDS:
Doncaster.
Scotland 29/12/28.
St Margarets 9/1/29.
Hatfield 25/11/30.
King's Cross 10/8/34.

RENUMBERED:
9592 10/8/46.
69592 15/7/49.

CONDEMNED: 23/9/61.
Into Don. for cut up 23/9/61.

2687

Yorkshire Engine Co. 2225.

To traffic 10/1/29.

REPAIRS:
Don. 27—29/12/28.**L.**
Cow. 11—17/1/29.**L.**
Cow. 24/8—20/10/31.**G.**
Don. 24/10—23/12/31.**L.**
Condensing and trip cock gear fitted.
Don. 13/9—4/11/33.**G.**
Don. 19/7—30/8/35.**G.**
Don. 1/7—14/8/37.**G.**
Don. 15/5—17/6/39.**G.**
Don. 16/12/41—31/1/42.**G.**
Don. 14/4—13/6/46.**G.**
Don. 4/10—23/11/48.**G.**
Don. 22/2—19/3/51.**G.**
Don. 8/8—14/9/53.**G.**
Don. 18/1—25/2/56.**G.**

No.895 seems to have kept LNER from its 26th October 1940 shopping, this not being disturbed by Cowlairs when ex-works 20th November 1943. On Sunday 5th May 1946 Parkhead changed it to 9565 in shaded transfers.

Between 26th January 1946 (4608/9492) and 9th January 1947 (4745/9524 also 4748/9527) the whole class was re-numbered 9490 to 9596. Most were done at their sheds and 12in. painted figures seem to have been used, no case of 6in. stencils having been found.

Just one N2 managed to get green lined livery during the LNER's post-war attempt to get away from black. Ex-Doncaster 9th November 1946, No.9522 had green, which it kept until going into works on 15th May 1949 for its next repair. Neasden shed, August 1947.

When No.9516 was ex-works on 21st April 1947, Doncaster was already running out of shaded transfers and yellow painted and unshaded Gill sans letters and figures were put on. Note that the 6 and 9 were an LNER modified version of correct Gill sans.

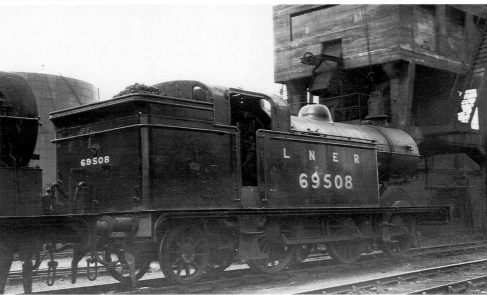

But Cowlairs were able to find shaded transfers for No.69508, ex-works on 17th April 1948 with BR numbers but still lettered LNER. Note number on back of bunker still applied in NBR style. Kipps shed, April 1948.

No.69508 was an oddity, being the only one seen with a smokebox numberplate on the lower part of the door. Eastfield, September 1954.

2687 cont./
Don. 22/12/58—5/2/59.**G.**

BOILERS:
8138.
8134 30/8/35.
8094 14/8/37.
9149 17/6/39.
9179 13/6/46.
9060 23/11/48.
21252 19/3/51.
21470 14/9/53.
21459 25/2/56.
21208 5/2/59.

SHEDS:
Doncaster.
Scotland 10/1/29.
Haymarket 21/1/29.
King's Cross 24/10/31.
Hitchin 8/6/42.
King's Cross 25/5/47.
New England 20/5/62.

RENUMBERED:
9593 13/6/46.
69593 20/11/48.

CONDEMNED: 16/9/62.
Into Don. for cut up 21/2/63.

2688

Yorkshire Engine Co. 2226.

To traffic 17/1/29.

REPAIRS:
Don. 7—10/1/29.**L.**
Cow. 18—19/1/29.**L.**
Cow. 4/12/30—16/1/31.**G.**
Don. 18/3—14/6/33.**G.**
Don. 15/11—14/12/35.**G.**
Don. 14/10—6/11/37.**G.**
Don. 28/4—19/5/38.**L.**
Don. 24/2—4/4/40.**G.**
Don. 17/4—11/8/43.**G.**
Don. 13/10—7/12/45.**G.**
Don. 5/1—12/2/48.**G.**

Don. 5/7—3/8/50.**G.**
Don. 24/7—21/8/53.**G.**
Don. 1/8—1/9/56.**G.**

BOILERS:
8139.
8285 14/12/35.
9264 11/8/43.
8136 12/2/48.
9223 3/8/50.
21468 21/8/53.
21305 1/9/56.

SHEDS:
Doncaster.
Scotland 17/1/29.
St Margarets 19/1/29.
Ardsley 19/1/31.
Bradford 11/2/31.
Copley Hill 9/5/37.
Bradford 29/7/38.
King's Cross 27/9/41.
Hatfield 7/12/41.
Hornsey 21/3/54.
Hitchin 12/7/59.

RENUMBERED:
9594 21/7/46.
ᴇ9594 12/2/48.
69594 3/8/50.

CONDEMNED: 2/1/60.
Into Don. for cut up 2/1/60.

2689

Yorkshire Engine Co. 2227.

To traffic 12/3/29.

REPAIRS:
Don. 20/2—23/2/29.**L.**
(Cowlairs records missing).
Cow. ?/?—?/12/31.**G.**
Dar. 18—27/4/32.**N/C.**
Raven FSA fitted.
Cow. 14/4—19/5/34.**G.**
Cow. ?/?—20/9/35.**G.**
Cow. ?/?—1/5/37.**H.**

Cow. ?/?—22/6/37.**L.**
Cow. ?/?—29/6/37.**L.**
Cow. ?/?—4/11/39.**G.**
Cow. ?/?—15/3/41.**G.**
Cow. ?/?—14/4/43.**G.**
Cow. ?/?—12/10/43.**L.**
Cow. 27/1—10/2/45.**G.**
Cow. 3—25/10/46.**H.**
Westinghouse brake removed.
Cow. 21/3—30/4/49.**G.**
Cow. 16—20/1/50.**N/C.**
Cow. 6—8/3/50.**C/L.**
Cow. 4—13/1/51.**C/L.**
Cow. 5—24/3/51.**L/I.**

Cow. 1—7/11/51.**C/L.**
Cow. 26—28/5/52.**N/C.**
Cow. 7/6—10/7/54.**G.**
Cow. 14/7/54.**N/C.**
Cow. 18/9—19/10/56.**L/I.**
Cow. 17/9/57. Not repaired.

BOILERS:
8140.
8140 reno.C1707 ?/12/31.
C1681 (ex2586) 4/11/39.
C1670 (ex2586) 10/2/45.
1381 (ex9563) 30/4/49.
1381 reno.21541 24/3/51.
21548 (exD1 62209) 10/7/54.

SHEDS:
Doncaster.
Eastfield 12/3/29.
Dundee by 11/8//30.
Eastfield by 10/1/31.
Gateshead 25/12/31.
Kipps 28/6/33.
Parkhead 4/7/33.

RENUMBERED:
9595 30/6/46.
69595 30/4/49.

CONDEMNED: 19/10/57.
Cut up at Kilmarnock 11/57.

2690

Yorkshire Engine Co. 2228.

To traffic 20/3/29.

REPAIRS:
Don. 2/3—12/3/29.**L.**
(Cowlairs records missing).
Cow. ?/?—3/2/32.**H.**
Dar. 11—14/7/32.**N/C.**
Raven FSA fitted.
Cow. 6/1—1/2/34.**G.**
Cow. 18/4—11/7/36.**G.**
Cow. ?/?—3/9/36.**L.**
Cow. ?/?—4/3/38.**G.**
Cow. ?/?—20/7/40.**G.**
Cow. ?/?—27/6/42.**L.**
Cow. 8/8—5/9/42.**G.**
Cow. ?/?—24/5/43.**L.**
Cow. ?/?—1/7/44.**G.**
Cow. 23/4—30/5/47.**G.**
Cow. 5/1—12/2/49.**H/I.**
Cow. 22/2—17/3/50.**L/I.**
Cow. 2—19/10/50.**C/H.**
Cow. 19/11—19/12/53.**G.**

BOILERS:
8141.
8141 reno.C1708 3/2/32.
1383 (ex895) 1/2/34.
8109 (exDon.) 5/9/42.
1383 30/5/47.
21532 (ex69565) 19/12/53.

SHEDS:
Doncaster.
Eastfield 20/3/29.
Gateshead 5/2/32.
Kipps 15/12/32.

RENUMBERED:
9596 30/6/46.
69596 12/2/49.

CONDEMNED: 2/9/60.
Cut up at Cowlairs 29/10/60.

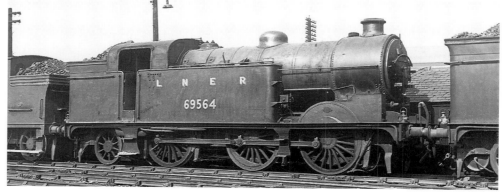

Cowlairs continued to leave LNER undisturbed when its condition allowed. From a light repair 12th January 1950 No.69564 had its BR number but still on the tank and under LNER in shaded transfers. This display was retained until 69564 went for repair on 25th September 1954. Note the unusual cover at base of safety valves. Parkhead shed, March 1950.

The first sign of new owners came on 6th February 1948 when Nos.E9498 and E9504 were out with 7½in. lettering on the tank and the number moved to the bunker. Four more were put into this style during the early months of 1948: E9594 (12th February), and in March E9557 (2nd), E9591 (12th) and E9559 (16th). Doncaster works, April 1949.

No.E9498 as repaired at Doncaster 6th February 1948 with the number moved to the bunker and trip cock moved to within 5ft. of the leading coupled axle.

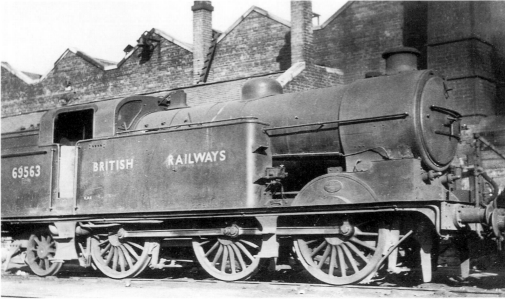

From Cowlairs it was on the 12th June 1948 before the new style appeared and the lettering was well above the centre of the tank. No.69563 was still in this guise to 1st August 1955.

Although Doncaster changed from E to 6 prefix from mid-March 1948 they continued with 12in. numbers on the bunker. No.69582 was ex-works 31st May 1948.

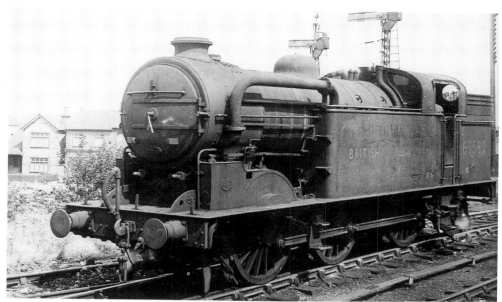

By 4th August 1948, when No.69586 was ex-works, Doncaster was using 9in. numbering and in the same style as Cowlairs but centred on the tank and bunker. No.69567 (see page 109, top) had the 9in. figures when out 7th July 1948.

Whilst still using unlined black, Doncaster changed to 10in. which became standard for letters and numbers. They also corrected the 6 and 9 to true Gill sans both on the bunker and on the smokebox numberplate. No.69550 was ex-works 2nd June 1949.

When ex-Cowlairs 12th June 1948, No.69563 had number on the front buffer beam and this was retained when the smokebox numberplate was put on at a light repair 13th November 1949. Parkhead shed, July 1953.

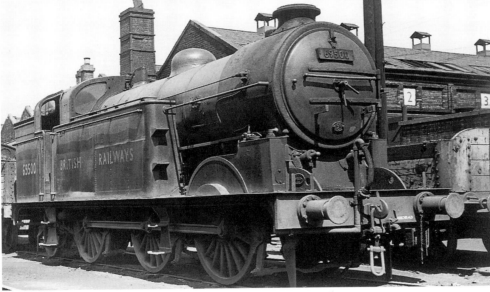

By 28th September 1948, when No.69500 was ex-Cowlairs, the lower position for lettering and figures had been adopted. A smokebox plate was put on and all those cast at Cowlairs had the correct 6 and 9. Note the strengthened fixing for coupling hook. Eastfield, June 1950.

(below) From No.69596, out 12th February 1949, Cowlairs began to apply standard BR red, cream and grey lining whilst still using the lettering. Kipps shed, June 1949.

For inclusion in the exhibition of locomotives in Doncaster plant on 17th and 18th July 1948, to mark the visit of the Railway Queen, No.69580 was given the new standard BR lining but had modified 6 and 9 on the plate and on the bunker. It went back to traffic 21st July 1948.

(below) Doncaster did not put lining on any others until No.69542 was done 20th August 1949 (see page 72, bottom) in anticipation of change from letters to emblem. No.69551 out 4th October and 69547 out 7th November 1949 had emblem and lining which were then applied as standard at repainting, until early 1956.

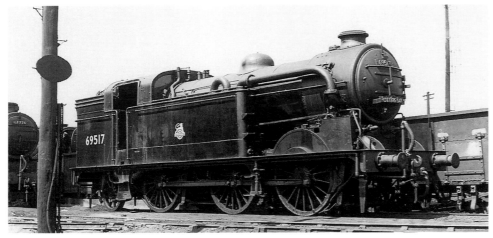

Ex-Stratford 7th April 1956, No.69576 and 69517 out 26th April, were again unlined. King's Cross, May 1956.

Doncaster too did not apply lining to all their output, No.69529 out on 19th May 1956 being plain black. Note modified 6 and 9 on the smokebox plate, this having been fitted on 18th June 1948. Doncaster shed, May 1956.

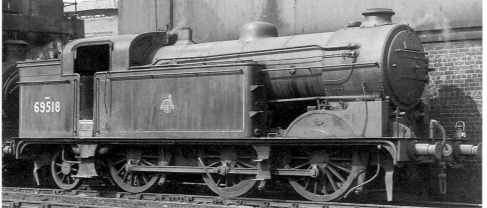

Painted at Cowlairs 20th January 1950, No.69518 got the emblem and lining but still had the modified 6 and 9 which it did not lose until it went for repair on 8th February 1955. Kipps shed, August 1954.

Ex-Doncaster 18th May 1957, No.69589 had full lining and had been changed to the new BR crest. Doncaster shed, 19th May 1957.

No.69582 got lining and crest when ex-Stratford 14th December 1957. On the right hand side the crest was heraldically wrong with the lion facing to the right and 69582 never had it corrected as its next works visit in September 1960 was for cutting up at Doncaster. Thirty-six got the crest and those which had the wrong example never had it changed. Doncaster works, 23rd October 1960.

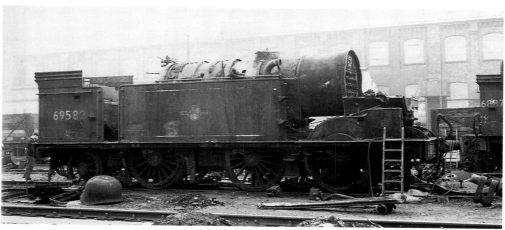

No.69504 changed from emblem to crest when ex-Doncaster on 5th March 1959 and by then the acceptable version of the crest was being used. No.69579 out 6th November 1958 and 69538 out 13th November 1958 had the correct version. Only four others: Nos.69529, 69546, 69568 and 69581, done subsequently, would have the correct crest.

From Cowlairs only two, Nos.69507 (24th August 1957) and 69510 (19th April 1958), are believed to have had the crest put on.

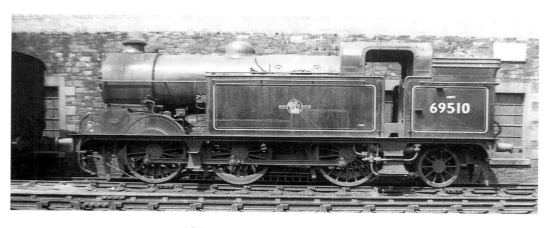

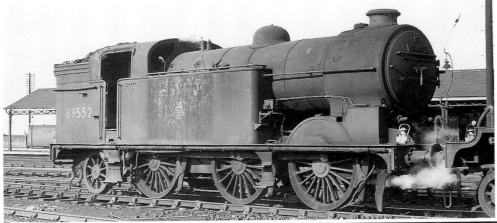

No.69552 got full lining when out from a general repair at Doncaster on 13th March 1953. However, it was not so favoured at its next general repair because when out of Stratford on 24th March 1956, it was plain black and remained so until withdrawn on 9th May 1960. Grantham, 26th August 1959.

No.4724 was a permanent transfer to Scottish Area from 1st August 1927 but before it went into traffic on 6th December 1927, from Dunfermline shed, it visited Cowlairs works to have a Westinghouse brake fitted, and the top coal rail removed. Eastfield shed.

No.4724 became 9503 on 31st March 1946 when ex-Cowlairs from a general repair in which the Westinghouse brake was taken off. On 3rd January 1957 it was withdrawn still as shown in this August 1956 photograph. After almost 30 years away from the London district it still had tall double lamp iron, GN destination board brackets, handrail below top hinge strap, right hand drive and Ramsbottom safety valves. Aberdeen Ferryhill shed, August 1956.

The only green painted LNER N2 did not thus survive its next repair for which it entered Doncaster on 15th May 1949. Out on 10th June 1949, it was plain black but with correct Gill sans 6 and 9 both on the bunker and smokebox plate. Doncaster shed.

No.69567, ex-Doncaster 7th July 1948, with smokebox numberplate with the LNER modified 6 and 9 which Doncaster used for the early plate castings. Hornsey shed.

(below) No.69511 on 2nd August 1960 at Dawsholm shed from which it was withdrawn on 15th December 1960. Details to note are toe hole in cab entrance, rectangular cover at base of safety valve and curious shape of anti-vacuum valve.

After its 16th September 1962 withdrawal, No.69523 stood at New England shed until received for scrap at Doncaster works on 13th February 1963. It was purchased by the Gresley Society for preservation and on 18th November 1963 it was moved from the works to Carr locomotive shed. On 19th November it was hauled in the 5.35 a.m. Doncaster Decoy to Harworth colliery and stored there (as here) until 26th February 1965 when it was hauled to Scrooby and attached to 8F76 special train Ranskill to Keighley consisting of Lancashire & Yorkshire 0-6-0 No.957, Locomotive Stores van No.95305 and the N2.

(above) **The final leg from Keighley to Haworth was on Saturday 6th March 1965 when the N2 was hauled by another ex-GNR engine, 0-6-0T No.1247. No.4744's first run in steam on the Worth Valley line was on Saturday 31st July 1965 to bring rolling stock from Keighley and then in passenger service.**

(left) **The following ten years were served either in use or as a static exhibit on the Keighley & Worth Valley Railway. Note the short rail high on the smokebox door was not altered. In November 1975 No.4744 was moved to the Great Central Railway (*see* Introduction).**